STRAIT GATE

To Gerda Wilson

Because of Calvary —

Agnes Rodli

STRAIT GATE

**A NORSE SAGA:
MISSION TO THE DIOMEDE
ISLANDS IN THE 1920'S**

Agnes Rodli

Cover art by
Bill Stewart
Ketchikan, Alaska

WINEPRESS WP PUBLISHING

Printed in the United States of America

Packaged by WinePress Publishing, PO Box 428, Enumclaw, WA 98022. The views expressed or implied in this work do not necessarily reflect those of WinePress Publishing. Ultimate design, content, and editorial accuracy of this work are the responsibilities of the author.

Unless otherwise noted all scriptures are taken from the King James Version of the Bible.
\

ISBN 1-57921-198-4
Library of Congress Catalog Card Number: 99-63243

Acknowledgments

Delving into the not-too-distant past became an adventure, putting me in touch with people who helped expand the original account of mission work on Little Diomede in the 1920s. We are especially indebted to members of the Nyseter family, as well as to Sigurd Breimoen of Norway, who gave us free use of reprinted material. The Slavic Mission Society of Stockholm also furnished valuable information.

Mildred Sarv, whose husband, Paul, served as boatman on the ill-fated *Ariel,* knew key people in the story, adding personal touches which otherwise might have been lost. Not least, Victor Carlsen, who, after a year on Little Diomede, ministered with the shantymen in camps and isolated communities of British Columbia, shared from his treasure of experience.

When I got bogged down with Norwegian, nephew Steve Rodli (who also gave the book its title) gently escorted me back to English. To the above and the many others, including public libraries who helped preserve fragments of history enacted in this little-known corner of Alaska, Thank You!

Contents

Preface

What did Gustav Nyseter know when he first responded to God's call on his life? Only this, that one day he would leave Norway and go to the ends of the earth. These he later pulled together off the coast of Alaska where two continents are narrowly separated by the Bering Strait and the international date line. On Little Diomede, an island encompassing barely more than two square miles, the twenty-four-hour calendar period closes. A scant two miles west lays Russian-owned Big Diomede, where a new day—or perhaps better said, a different day—begins.

After several years on the smaller rock and in close contact with natives of the Russian Far East (Pacific Maritime Siberia), Nyseter returned to Norway. There, drawing from his journal and letters, he wrote *Jordens Ytterste Ender* (Earth's Farthest Ends), describing his years with a people bound by fear and superstition. Though referring to an adverse culture, he spoke with honesty and charity—imperative in view of his own ancestry, Viking stock that could hardly be classed as holy men of old.

Laura and Gustav Nyseter, twentieth-century emissaries of good will to the north, had much in common with David Livingstone, nineteenth-century explorer-missionary to Africa, who purportedly spoke with prophet's ken: "We are voices crying in the wilderness; we prepare the way for a glorious future. Future missionaries will be rewarded with conversions for every sermon. We are their pioneers and helpers. Let them not forget the watchmen of the night—us, who worked when all was gloom, and no evidence of success in the way of conversion cheered our paths. They will doubtless have more light than we; but we can serve Our Master earnestly and proclaim the Gospel as they will do."

Of such mettle was Nyseter who penned both joys and hardships—and displayed a firm confidence that God would complete the work He had entrusted them to begin. Of necessity I rewrote much of his book in the third person, expanding it with historical information relevant to our day. But when it came to the man's self portrayal, I tried not to lose a word, for few people have bared their deepest inner feelings as he did. You will agree that these were too sacred for me to alter in any way.

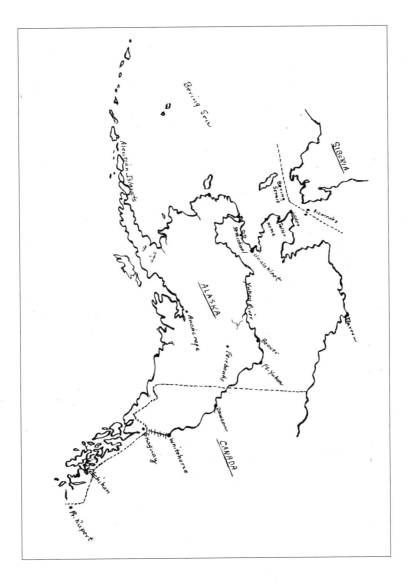

1

The Call

=◆=

Y ears of waiting and then the all-too-hurried good-
byes.
"This way," the police escort ordered.
The year: 1921. Place: Norway in the midst of post-war
adjustments. Though not a young nation, she had begun
with uncertain steps to walk on her own after severing a
century-long treaty with Sweden in 1905. To fill the quali-
fications of a full-fledged monarchy, she offered the throne
to Denmark's Prince Haakon. He accepted. The country's
first economic boon came with World War I when both
sides of that great conflict needed fish and farm products.

As those exports phased out, the inevitable happened.
A population shift from small farms to larger towns erupted
in labor disputes and other demands of the working class.
But the troubles besetting this land of majestic mountains
and peaceful fjords were not Gustav and Laura Nyseter's
reason for leaving. Rather, they were driven by a sense of
purpose that promised no rest until fulfilled.

Ignoring heated tempers picketing the docks, the police officer threaded would-be travelers through guarded areas and to the passenger vessel *Rollo* bound for Liverpool and ports beyond. A shipping strike wouldn't keep them from sailing on schedule.

Leaving carry-on luggage in their rooms, the Nyseters hurried back on deck, straining to get a glimpse of family and friends who had come to Kristiania (now Oslo) to see them off. When sailors at last began hauling in the heavy ropes holding the ship to the wharf, the couple waved frantically. Perhaps someone in that milling crowd would spot them and pass along those final farewells.

As night lowered, they lingered, longing for one more distant glimpse of the snowcapped peaks of their beloved Norway. Gone. Now to their narrow compartment....

How had they gotten this far from home? For Gustav, the journey began back in August 1908, when his widowed mother pried his secret from him. The twenty-two-year-old hadn't meant to admit being troubled, but the broken rhythm of his ax coming down on rounds of northern pine betrayed him. Pauses were too frequent. Balancing a round on the chopping block, only to turn it first one way and then another before swinging a final blow, he stalled for time. How can one give an answer when he isn't sure of the question?

The Nyseter family home lay in Østerdalen, a forested region of south-central Norway, where the customary eight years of the three R's plus history and geography comprised the average child's schooling. After that, a lad was expected to follow in his father's footsteps unless he could apprentice in a chosen vocation. By honing his skills and talents, Gustav could have qualified as either a builder or a writer, both of which would put *kroner* (crowns) in his pocket. But was that what he really wanted? A nudge toward another calling kept him from pursuing those courses.

The state church had supplied religious instruction in the public school, their catechism providing a sound theological base. The youth could borrow precious books from the parish priest to enlarge his understanding of Scripture, and that's what interested him most. So at age twenty-one he set his life's course with, "Whatever you want, Lord."

Whatever. While further formal education remained out of the question for one born into his family's income level, Gustav latched on to a role he could fill. Current social and economic changes were already sending ripples into the religious framework of his nation. More home study groups as well as evangelistic outreach within the organized church grew while an exodus toward "free" congregations gradually gained momentum.

Observing these trends, Gustav stepped forward to do what he saw best at the time. He responded to invitations to give solid Bible instruction in surrounding communities. Ah, this was it! With a sense of duty—nonetheless with pleasure—he shared what he learned, and was learning, with whomever would listen.

Fru Nyseter looked on with an allowable measure of pride. It wouldn't surprise her if her son told her that he must go farther afield. He needed to extend his opportunities. It wouldn't be easy for her either, but the other relatives and friends would look after her.

With both tenderness and a measure of apprehension, she ventured, "Your future, Son. What are you thinking?"

In that instant, a ray of sunlight burst over the now-awakening call that had rested over him for months. Though certain, it nonetheless lacked specifics. After a pause, he answered quietly, "I only know this, Mother, that the Lord will send me to the ends of the earth."

There! Out of his own mouth scattered thoughts—sometimes plaguing, sometimes eluding—took shape. The ends of the earth. That meant going to Africa, of course—unless it was China or India, places where missionaries usually went. Anyway, for sure it would be south, down where the climate is hot and sticky, where people died from fevers and flies. Dying by the millions. Though eager to face the challenge, Gustav struggled to envision himself in a jungle or in the Orient. The picture always clicked off. Gradually a new scene emerged: ice and snow. He felt puzzled, the description fitting neither Lapland nor Finnmark in north Norway.

"While an inner nudging kept reminding me of Eskimos," he later confessed, "I tried to stifle the thought of going to the cold, forbidding regions where they lived. How could I explain that to my friends? And how in the world would I get there? Other missionaries could help me get to Africa, but to Eskimoland? Surely there was some place less lonely. There had to be."

With that, the young man returned to the near at hand. Study groups and fledgling churches hearing of his teaching ability called him. When earth's farthest ends did manage to push through his subconscious, he put them back in God's hand with a question he borrowed from Moses. Taken somewhat out of context, he quoted it anyway, "You have never said whom you will send with me."

Surely he wouldn't be going alone. Maybe he and another young man could become a Paul-and-Silas team. He'd like to go one better, a Priscilla-and-Aquila team, if he could please find his Priscilla.

After making several evangelistic tours through central and south Norway, Gustav traveled north and west to the region of Norland. There he met an attractive blonde, a Bible teacher who had come from a community about fifty kilometers above Bode. With typical Norwegian reserve, he later described Laura Volden as "a young lady who impressed me as no one else ever had. It wasn't long until we both realized that God meant us for each other."

As an apparent confirmation of God's call, Laura also had sensed an underlying conviction that she would be going to the ends of the earth. But neither could she pinpoint a certain country and thus proceed in a given direction. It took much prayer before they could admit to themselves that they were indeed destined for ministry among Eskimo people.

"After we were married," Gustav wrote in his diary, "we determined to lose no more time getting on our way. Laura and I concluded quite logically that our assignment meant going to Greenland, which belonged to Denmark."

The young couple congratulated themselves on not having to struggle with years of language study. While in the process of learning Greenlandic, they could get by with Danish, its spelling being similar to Norwegian. Due to differences in pronunciation, however, Danish ridden with a Norwegian accent might require some patient listening for a while. Never mind—that wasn't the worst. The road ahead looked easy.

With high hopes, the Nyseters journeyed to Copenhagen to confer with proper authorities. To their dismay they were advised that registration of births, marriages, and similar duties along with the religious training of Greenlanders lay under the jurisdiction of the Danish state church. The young couple couldn't so much as fill out initial applications. A heavy door creaked shut behind them.

Within minutes they stood again on the cold marble stairs, looking at each other nonplused. "It can't be," they reasoned, "because God makes no mistakes."

If not His mistake, then whose? Could they have misunderstood their calling when, pressed by their burden for the Eskimo, they presumed Greenland? After admitting that strong possibility, they opened their minds to further direction, and gradually thoughts of Alaska seeped in—exciting, but scary. In practical fashion, Gustav evaluated their position: "We really aren't equipped to handle everything involved, nor do we have the financial backing for that kind of travel. I guess we'll begin all over again."

Feeling a bit embarrassed, the couple reluctantly retraced their route home to explain their obvious jumping to conclusions. They would still be going to the Eskimo, but at a later date as missionaries to America. They might not have recognized it right away, but the setback served a definite purpose. These small-town Norwegians with almost no understanding of foreign cultures needed to get their feet wet. Phase one began with accepting invitations to isolated communities deep in the fjords.

There, customs changed. Entrenched in an earlier belief were the cute/ugly little trolls that parade the shelves of souvenir shops today. These were, however, still an actuality in the minds of those who lived far from nearest neighbors. When people flatly stated that they heard those mini-devils in the night, they meant it. Trolls served a purpose. If something happened for which there was no quick logical explanation, they were there to receive the blame. Superstitions wove themselves into the fabric of everyday living. So what if imagination ran wild? It made for chilling stories—all the better if accented by a shrill wind whistling around the corner of the house on a stormy night. Prayer for protection from "things that go bump in the night" didn't qualify as an Irish joke when winter's dark hours outnumbered the light. These were very real factors that the missionaries-in-training had to understand and learn to deal with.

Finally in the spring of 1921, with the Nyseters in their midthirties and seasoned enough to meet new cultural challenges, the all clear sounded for them to proceed on their way.

2

Westward

—◆—

The old saying about anticipation being greater than realization applies first-class to an ocean voyage third-class—sheer monotony both indoors and out when weather turns foul. Fog and heavy seas surrounded the Nyseters' ship all the way, their brief layover in England just that—a brief layover. The second lap held a bit more adventure when they nearly rammed an iceberg. Mostly, however, they met relentless waves head on, up and down, night and day until they reached the fresh waters of St. Lawrence River.

Quebec, here we come! How inviting the city looked to the weary travelers! And they could hardly wait to exchange ocean swells for the solidity of steel rail. Too soon spoken. The trade-off meant swaying sideways to the tune of clacking wheels while enduring scorching heat from the afternoon sun. One compensation—they came in contact with other Scandinavians who instructed them in money changing, ordering meals, and other important dos and don'ts for getting along in the new world.

At Winnipeg, Manitoba, passengers continuing westward had to change trains. The shuffle snatched the Nyseters away from their new acquaintances and slapped them down on their own. The full impact of being foreigners hit Gustav and Laura hard when the station manager pulled them back every time they tried to board another car. Hours later they finally understood that their line wouldn't move until the next day. So that was the problem!

Laura, who had always enjoyed the best of health, had to admit she wasn't meant to be a sailor. Hanging over the rail at sea, followed by nausea from an opposite kind of motion on land, left her too weak to cope with the stifling heat of the prairies. For both of them, drained energy begged a night's sleep in a real bed.

"Wait here in the station, and I'll find us a room," Gustav said as he set out with long strides, hoping to meet a policeman who could to help them. There were enough hotels, Gustav concluded as he spelled out *H-o-t-e-l*, the same as the word back home. He passed them by, fearful lest his bungled inquiry lead to costly accommodations. They wanted only a room and a cooked meal, perhaps in a mission, some place where he could make himself understood....

Absorbed in thought, Gustav was taken totally by surprise when a man in uniform greeted him, "*Er du Norsk, du?* [Aren't you Norwegian?] *Jeg er Svensk.* [I am Swedish.]"

The newcomer stood amazed. Then words tumbled out in his mother tongue...yes, from Norway...his wife with the baggage at the station...they needed a room for the night.

Surely this was a miracle from God—meeting the only Scandinavian officer on the Winnipeg police force, one who recognized him as a Norwegian! The first part qualified as a miracle, but the second? Gustav's clothing, his self-conscious manners, and even his stride proclaimed a stranger from a land of hills and valleys. Almost anyone could have guessed that. The officer directed him to a kind Baptist brother who owned a restaurant and rented rooms as well.

"It wasn't long until I stood at Brother Mieyer's desk, where I introduced myself and asked for lodging," Gustav wrote. "Brother Mieyer did far more, going with me to the station to get my wife and our belongings. Then he invited us to dinner, after which his family insisted we stay with them for several days to rest up. They also asked me to speak in their meetings where God gave beautiful liberty in proclaiming His Word. Our days with them became a chapter of pleasant memories. When we were ready to get on our way again, a little flock of newfound friends assembled on the station platform to wish us Godspeed."

The Nyseters were off to a fine start with earlier immigrants often standing by ready to help. If these events were indicative of the route which lay before them, they had it made!

The sweltering heat of the plains eased off when their train entered the Rocky Mountain Pass, gateway to the Pacific. The cool autumn air, however, came with a shock almost more than Laura could take. By the time they reached the end of the line at Prince Rupert, British Columbia, sitting up had become a painful effort. Again Gustav had to find someone who could decipher his homespun combination of signs and sounds. Bolstered by previous heartwarming experiences, he started out and quickly found the right contacts.

It took another week for Gustav to secure ship's passage as well as clear with the immigration office before proceeding on to American territory. Much to their delight, the Norwegian consulate not only assisted them in travel matters but also took them out to dinner. That was one to write home about!

Recognizing the Nyseters' willingness to share their faith, the Christian community suggested that they settle in Prince Rupert and begin a ministry among their own people. The couple appreciated the vote of confidence, but "*Ney, tak* [No, thank you]." A prior commitment farther north held firm.

3

Southeast Alaska

Their Alaska-bound ship sailed a number of hours north and west along a forested coastline cut with deep inlets until it reached what interior Alaskans termed *southeast*. Near the tip of the panhandle lay the fishing town of Ketchikan. After fifteen years of looking forward to stepping ashore on the land of their calling, the weary travelers experienced a letdown. The big moment: Independence Day with flags flying, or at least flopping, but the flags weren't for them.

As Gustav later confessed, "We weren't in the least impressed. Instead of taking in the thrill of at last standing on Uncle Sam's soil, we huddled in the drizzling rain with our vision focused on muddy streets. To make matters worse, the very thought of journeying on made Laura ill.

"Someone directed us to a *Norsk* [Norwegian] hotel that evening, but one night was hardly enough. By the next day we faced facts squarely: Laura's health told us to put roots down for a while. Though frustrated by yet another delay, we later recognized the Lord's wisdom in halting our eager plans. Whatever could we have done up north without first acquiring a working knowledge of the English language?"

So began their introduction to "the Great Land" and Alaskan hospitality. Without anyone implying that they needed to get Americanized, their eyes caught an important announcement—an evening course in English offered by one of the local professors. Gustav and Laura quickly enrolled and later caught on that they often sat as the only two students. Seeing through the ploy, they smiled. The townsfolk's obvious concern rated as one of the warmest welcome mats ever placed under their feet.

By spring they had settled in comfortably enough to begin considering options other than going farther north. Skilled with his hands, Gustav picked up enough jobs to help them get ahead; outlets for ministry multiplied. On Sundays, Gustav went to the jail to witness to a captive audience that listened politely, never making fun of this outsider who got his v's and w's mixed up. If his broken English amused them, they never let on. Besides, what that preacher practicing on them said made a lot of sense.

As a special treat, the Nyseters went with a tour group to visit Metlakatla, an Indian settlement south of Ketchikan. Coming from a culture that emphasizes keeping their cemeteries attractive, the couple was most impressed by a grave without monument or inscription. It needed none. For these responsible people, their church, sawmill, boat building, and other signs of progress constituted the finest epitaph a person could hope for—a perpetual memorial. Under a small plot rested the remains of William Duncan, a man who gave sixty years of his life to the Tsimshian people.

Duncan, a Scottish lay preacher and former dry goods clerk, went to Canada's west coast under the auspices of the Anglican Church in 1857. He immediately began studying the language and soon established a model community. Later he asked permission to do a similar work in Alaska. Duncan died in 1898, but village leaders of the Metlakatla Indian Mission continued the work he had begun.

"Laying the right foundation," Gustav concluded, "is what it's all about." Although there would be no lumber mill to build in the barren north, he determined to do as this hero had done—walk side by side with the converts God gave him.

Then came another invitation to cancel further travel when in the spring of 1922 the wife of a Norwegian who held an important position in the town died. Concerned that his small boys have the best of care under godly influence, the widower asked the Nyseters to move in with him. He would hire Laura as housekeeper, Gustav as one of his assistants.

They wanted to help this brother, but was that what they were supposed to do? Their countrymen, of course, tried their best to persuade them to accept the offer. Could they not see the finger of God in this sudden turn of events? Besides, the poor Eskimos up north possibly wouldn't understand (much less appreciate) their living among them. The couple wavered to the point of almost abandoning their call to the ends of the earth. Only after hours of prayer did they get back on track again, convinced that God had not changed His mind.

How did Gustav and Laura arrive at their decision to move on? "The cloud lifted itself—our signal to break camp," he wrote. "Like the Old Testament believers leaving Egypt, we got our clue, for 'when the cloud was taken up from over the tabernacle, the children of Israel went onward in all their journeys'" (Exod. 40:36).

Without the slightest hint as to what for them constituted "the cloud," Gustav wound up his journal entry: "Like migratory birds, we instinctively knew that we were able to surmount whatever hardships were entailed in moving and resettling again in a strange land. We were confident of a sure Hand directing us ever onward."

4

Onward

⟞⟝

Like the migratory birds of which Gustav spoke, a stop-and-go route to north Alaska lay before them. Sailing through the Aleutian Chain and across the Bering Sea might have been quicker and less expensive, but without a remedy for Laura's seasickness...? That bordered on cruelty. Besides, Gustav recalled the outline of an overland map he had received in a vision back in Norway. Better follow it.

They booked passage the first part of June on a coastal vessel that wound through narrow passages and around lush wooded islands, occasionally brushing against small icebergs drifting toward the sea. Forty-eight hours later, they docked at Skagway, the only real "city" with streetcar tracks in Alaska's southeastern panhandle. It boasted of history too, Evangeline Booth of the Salvation Army having been there to preach to thousands of prospectors and miners. The settlement boomed not only during the gold rush but also for some time afterward because of a rail connection to Canada. Though the town faced inevitable decline, its leaders obviously tried to make permanent investments. Old buildings stood solid. Even the cemetery was worth seeing: close to the grave of the shootin' outlaw Soapy Smith, stands another monument in honor of the officer who gave his life to bring about justice on the frontier. Skagway had enough residents who wanted their community to be known as more than a "drinkin' hole."

After renting a room for two or three nights, the Nyseters located an independent Holiness group with its "Peniel Mission" outreach housed in a box-like storefront near the town center. A young Assemblies of God couple, Charles and Florence Personeus from the village of Klukwan, were filling in for the resident workers on leave. These missionaries, who seldom had the privilege of receiving other workers, gladly invited the newcomers to take part in their outreach meetings. Thus Gustav was initiated into the unique experience of hearing an interpreter take his somewhat limited English into another language.

Inasmuch as the Personeuses had also planned to travel by the narrow gauge White Pass and Yukon Railway to Whitehorse, Yukon Territory, the two couples got on together. Fortunately, the Americans, going for only a short visit, had little to carry. Personeus, surrounded by boxes and barrels belonging to the Nyseters, shook his head, "I can't believe this baggage! What in the world are you going to do with so much stuff?"

"The Lord said, 'earth's farthest ends' and there might not be much there. We got to be ready for anything," Gustav replied.

The trained pulled out from Skagway on a sunny morning just right for traveling over the mountains. A Norwegian conductor often sat with the Nyseters, naming points of interest, telling turn-of-the-century stories as they rolled along. At one of the stops, he plucked wildflowers and juniper branches for Laura, wakening memories of summertime back in the old country. The upward climb to a height of about five miles often switchbacked with seldom more than sixty feet in a straight line. Gustav described the landscape as grand and wild though not, he carefully noted in his journal, as beautiful as their homeland.

High in the mountains they edged along deep ravines and looked out the window straight down to green rivers foaming and cascading hundreds of feet directly below. Occasionally passengers caught glimpses of the old Klondike trail that gold-hungry prospectors had trudged two or three decades before. Untold numbers died of sickness, starvation, or exposure, and not a few drowned in the turbulent rivers. And then there was Dead Horse Gulch, where literally thousands of pack animals dropped to instant death. Not least, sin itself took a greedy toll—price as yet not estimated. Laura closed her eyes, the cost of that gold more than she wanted imprinted on her mind.

The train stopped at the Canada-Alaska boundary, where uniformed men checked the passengers' baggage and asked a few questions—a mere formality between friendly nations. Over the summit, the scenery changed to green hills, quiet streams, and mirror-still lakes decking the landscape.

The 116-mile ride ended in the afternoon at Whitehorse where Yukon River traffic begins. Though the Nyseters had counted on immediately boarding the wood-burning sternwheeler, navigation ran behind schedule due to low water and ice on the lakes. Both couples secured comfortable lodging before going back out on the street to hold an open-air meeting. The next day they said their farewells.

Gustav and Laura boarded the barge-like vessel with its flat bottom and light superstructure specifically designed for shallow water. The big wheel began to turn slowly, but not for long. The boat quivered, then shuddered to a complete standstill to avoid getting grounded on a sand bar. Easing ahead, it reached a place where the water measured two or three feet at the most. For a couple of miles the sternwheeler acted like a great dinosaur dragging its belly through the sand.

Hours passed. Sometimes the bow of the boat moved forward as intended; other times the back end with its enormous wheel took the lead, digging out a channel for itself. With only his patient wife to listen, Gustav—ever the Bible teacher—sermonized: "It's a vivid illustration of what the prophet Ezekiel meant when he talked about 'water to the ankles, the knees, and the loins.' And look, Laura, pretty soon we'll reach that lake where we'll have 'waters to swim in.'"

Right on! With the wheels picking up momentum, the captain turned the vessel around to push forward. Tracing the path of the Yukon, it twisted snakelike through seemingly endless tracts of wilderness and sparsely wooded areas. Where high water had cut sharply through the dirt banks, tufts of grass, hummocks, and scraggly clumps of willow looked as if they were trying to heal (or at least hide) those wounds. The travelers spotted a few lone native camps, most often vacated. The splashing of the wheel along with an occasional piercing whistle apparently scared off wild animals the travelers had hoped to see.

A couple days later, they stopped at Dawson City, in its heyday a social and commercial center for at least thirty thousand gold seekers. It now stood a "has been" with a population of a few hundred. Obviously no one felt inclined to remove the weatherworn advertisements of gala affairs that had once attracted crowds. Maybe the remaining citizens nourished an underlying hope that it would one day make its mark again.

A few miles after Dawson City, the silt-laden river crossed over to the Alaska side. Constantly fed by tributaries, its size swells to one of the largest rivers on the North American continent. Reaching its most northerly point just below the Arctic Circle, the Yukon makes a big bend before flowing in a southwesterly direction. At its fat, three-mile-wide elbow lies Fort Yukon, a village clustered around a modest church and hospital established by the Episcopal Church in 1869. The community, well worth the brief stop, also boasted a wireless telegraph station along with a number of frontier-style dwellings built of unpeeled logs. And sled dogs everywhere.

"Time's up. Everyone on board!"

Along toward bedtime the couple could see a burned off area in the distance, but presumed they wouldn't reach it for several hours. They pondered: Why not stretch out on their berths for a while? Seeing yet another small village which meant little to them personally seemed repetitious.

Suddenly they realized the captain was steering toward a settlement close at hand. Through their field glasses they made out something new to them—people with faces framed in fur, just as they had seen in pictures. Could it be? Having heard that they might stop for a few hours, Gustav and Laura hurried ashore as soon as the sternwheeler nudged against the riverbank.

They greeted some of the young folk who spoke English. Sure enough! These were Eskimos who had come the long way overland from top-of-the-world Barrow down to the village of Beaver three or four years before. The most recent group of settlers left their old home in April, walking an estimated six hundred miles before reaching Beaver the middle of August.

Farther north they had attended the Presbyterian mission. Here in the absence of both church and school, the parents did their best to homeschool their children. When offered printed tracts, they responded by saying that they too believed in Jesus. The younger folk readily interpreted for their seniors who wanted to know more about this friendly pair and their reason for coming to Alaska. In spite of broken English on both sides, communication never lacked. The encounter served as a shot in the arm for the Nyseters who, walking back to the boat, kept saying to each other, "These are our people." For the first time they could feel that they had, at least in part, arrived.

According to his map, Gustav estimated they had gone half way, and thus far the journey had been pleasant. River travel is relatively smooth and often they sat on deck enjoying the long days while storing up sunshine for winter nights sure to come.

After another twenty-four hours, those continuing the Yukon journey were ordered ashore. A different carrier would take them the next lap. The passengers waited on land twelve hours before being directed to an undersized motor boat. Fortunately, the passenger list had dwindled, so the transfer wasn't the worst. It provided ample space, but made the sternwheeler they left look like a luxury liner.

Around midnight they were moved once more, this time to an even smaller vessel, the *Anna*, to take them the rest of the way. Their thoughts? *"Here we go again, traveling like sardines."* To worsen matters, an advancing storm whipped up the waves, forcing a layover at the entrance of a small river.

Besides passengers and baggage, the old, overworked motor had to push a barge loaded with produce, mail sacks, and gold. The passengers' tickets included meals, but when provisions ran low, the skipper took the Nyseters and a Finnish couple with their little daughter to a trading post. While he went for more freight, they all checked in at the lodge because of the rain and cold—at their own expense. The little *Anna* came back the following day. By then more travelers had joined them, making a total of nine plus three crewmen. The Finnish woman assumed responsibility for meals, so at least that part went better than expected.

For lack of space, some had to sit on the barge. One night Laura and Gustav slept under the tarpaulin covering for the mail and sacks of furs—a situation barely tolerable. Heavy canvas shielded them from the rain, and their own blankets kept them warm, but the heavy smell of raw skins began to get to them.

"Loathsome," Gustav muttered, half to himself and half to Laura. "You know, we've been treated miserably. It doesn't say much for a company that would sell such means of transportation. With what they charged for our tickets, they certainly could have done better by us. The only thing good to say is that at least every chug of the motor is pushing us closer toward our goal."

"Our goal." Out of his own mouth! After years of looking forward, they had switched to grumbling about it. Enough said. With that they turned their thoughts upward, thanking God for the privilege of serving Him. These were only temporary inconveniences, and down the road—or down the river—they would look back and laugh at this ridiculous set of circumstances. They had each other and the Lord. What else did they need?

As they traveled farther down the Yukon, the landscape appeared even more flat and barren, sizable villages farther apart. Here and there they spotted small cabins or board floor tents, heartening signs of human habitation. The drone of the motor along with the sameness of scenery dulled their conversation until Laura asked, "Do you hear it?"

"Hear what?"

"Beautiful singing. Don't you hear it?"

Gustav shook his head. He didn't hear anything. Then he began listening. He did hear it—a tune he recognized. As he hummed along, Laura looked at him and smiled. She was hearing the same melody! What a reminder that they weren't alone, that God sends His angels as ministering spirits when His children need added assurance. Talk about compensations!

At one of the landings, the Finnish family got off the boat. Being the only woman left on board, it fell Laura's lot to fill in as cook. The first twenty-four hours, however, the smell of gas and the rolling water got the better of her, and she had to lie down. With the boat no longer pushing a barge in front of it, the imprisoned passengers were forced to share a place with the smoking motor. Though they could have gone ashore whenever the *Anna* stopped to handle freight, the pelting rain quenched any desire to leave their cell.

Near its mouth, the river widened until it looked like an inland sea, the wind picking up accordingly. The last few miles, where they came into salt water, the wind reached gale velocity, pitching and rolling the poor craft unmercifully. Gustav tried his best to hold the oil stove in place, but suddenly seasickness overwhelmed him. Let the stove slide where it will—his turn to hang over the rail!

A hard jolt—the boat had scraped against a rock. With that the motor choked and sputtered, stopping repeatedly from water in its line. Within sight of their destination, the *Anna* was being tossed about like a scrap of driftwood, losing two feet for every three gained. So, in fact their eighteen hundred miles could have a plus after it.

Save the reckoning for another time. There's a shout—the skipper hailing someone on land to catch the ropes. St. Michael at last!

Looking back, the Nyseters found the trip hard to relive in their minds. Monotonous details of the river ride slipped into oblivion, with some days totally wiped from their memories were it not for Gustav's meticulous journal entries.

"In one of our most trying times," Gustav wrote home, "The Lord reminded me of the apostle Paul. Shipwrecked...in journeying often...in perils of water...in perils in the wilderness...in weariness... (2 Cor. 11:23–27). Yet it is in the hardest places that we learn the fuller meaning of God's grace."

Did they want to repeat the river trip? No way! At the same time, they agreed that they wouldn't trade those two weeks for anything.

5

St. Michael

T hough not situated exactly at the mouth of the Yukon, for all practical purposes St. Michael marked the end of river travel. It likewise served as a stopping place for ocean going vessels during open season.

Realizing its strategic location, Governor Wrangell of the Russian Company had established a fort there in 1833, thirty-four years before Russia sold its vast holdings to the United States. The colony served as a base for exploration of the Yukon basin, which he believed to be rich in furs. Wrangell spearheaded arctic research, promoting whatever development he deemed advantageous. Though major investments were unquestionably mercenary, a clause in the company's charter provided for the support of secular education along with propagating the Russian Orthodox tradition. The encouragement of these avenues depended of course on those in positions of authority. To the company's credit, they advanced a number of strong leaders genuinely concerned with the welfare of the local people.

The sale of Alaska opened the door for other church groups. Arriving at St. Michael, however, the Nyseters were disappointed to see little left of earlier evangelistic efforts. Moreover, they had taken for granted that, being the end of June, they would enjoy the warmth of full summer. Instead, fatigued and needing to get acclimated, they shivered with cold even when wearing their heaviest coats.

Finding a house to rent was a snap. Many dwellings stood empty, ghostly reminders of a once thriving community. Business section: store, post office, and telegraph station. Churches: Roman Catholic and Russian Orthodox, the latter little more than a shadow cast from Russia's earlier territorial claim. In spite of daily goings on, the town wore a forlorn look with not a friendly tree breaking the marshy landscape. Years before, enterprising citizens had laid thick planks for sidewalks and some of the streets. Now, with the community in recession, no one bothered to repair the rotted planking, which made for dangerous walking after dark. Gustav reflected that the houses looking down on the streets and lanes seemed to lean toward one another as if to whisper confidentially that the old days had been better than these.

The couple often went for walks, getting acquainted with their new surroundings. They tried to view the scene positively, but one or the other would suddenly blurt out, "I can't believe it!" Their spirits revolted against the moral decay eating away at the core of the society. Nor did the town proper, which was more or less a white man's center, outshine the native settlements to either side. If ever a place needed renewal, both physical and spiritual, this did!

Many problems were passed down by early prospectors who had left a trail of bad habits. Filth, weakness, and disease helped pave its inroads. Of all fevers, a burning lust for gold (or what it can buy) hangs on the longest, and covetousness breeds hate. Liquor, both imported and home-brew, contributed to several murders and suicides just before the Nyseters arrived. Also, a steamship missing the main channel and veering too close to the opposite shore added to the toll. Waves tossed the vessel like a toy, clearing its deck of wares—a keg of strong drink included—which called for a party in full swing. By morning three bodies lay on the beach.

The Nyseters heard one expression too often—*Godforsaken.* The description, not exactly true, put fight in Gustav. He'd roll up his sleeves and tackle the devil single-handed if he had to. These people had to be set free! In an ongoing battle, he and Laura stood shoulder to shoulder with heroes of the faith who had passed that way before them and with those who were yet to follow.

One of the first days after getting settled in their new home, Gustav walked to the east side of town with his guitar. Stopping near a cluster of houses, he began to play and sing. Doors slowly opened, just wide enough for heads to peer out.

"No doubt more out of curiosity than admiration for the quality of music," he observed with a chuckle. "Then gradually some young people dared to venture out. No danger, so others followed. Soon voices joined me in singing, 'Nearer, My God, to Thee.'

"A few edged closer to see the words in my book. After several songs, I called to those standing at a distance, inviting them to join our outdoor congregation. I had something I wished to say. When they came within fair listening range, I explained how I had come a long way to tell people about the Savior. In closing I read from the Bible and spoke briefly."

A woman stepped forward to shake his hand, "Thank you for coming."

Her carefully chosen words let the gangly preacher know that at least one person understood his broken English and appreciated his efforts. Later he learned that she had been widowed shortly before they came. Her husband was shot, or may have shot himself, during an attempted jailbreak.

Gustav and Laura continued holding their outdoor meetings until weather decreed otherwise. After that they met in homes. Most of those attending the services had previous contact with Covenant missionaries who had taught them a number of songs, some of which they sang in Eskimo. How they managed to squeeze their polysyllabic words into a given melody would forever remain a mystery to Scandinavian ears! Occasionally someone gave a testimony in his native tongue—participation that delighted Gustav, though he understood only one word, *Jesus*.

For all her longing to share with their neighbors, Laura found it difficult to get used to the strange odors of a crowd in close quarters. Her reactions may have been caused by an allergy not understood at that time. Mixing with a group came easier for her husband who felt richly rewarded when complimented with, "You good Eskimo."

Summer, such as it was, sped by so quickly that a cold front moving in caught them unprepared. Their main source of fuel, driftwood free for the taking, lay several miles from the town. Improvising a semblance to the timber floats of Osterdalen where he had grown up, Gustav managed one cumbersome load. But it left him unsure about trying it again. What about peat moss? He and Laura tried to stack it as they had seen done in the old country. Early in the project they threw up their hands and quit. No way could that wet stuff dry out before snowfall.

Later, Gustav discussed their heating situation with the storekeeper, who suggested working together to get coal from a site many miles up the coast. Needing a fair amount for his own use, he hired two men to dig coal for him; Gustav could dig his own. The storekeeper also agreed to haul their coal with his motor boat, but on different runs as his home lay in the opposite direction.

So came the dark night when, after several soaking hours at sea, the three workmen were put ashore with waves dashing high. This spot far from any other dwellings had a small hut with a stove in it. After building a roaring fire, the men hung their outer clothing to dry while they slept. For the next two days they dug feverishly. Gustav chalked up eighteen sacks of coal. Never mind that it lacked quality, for he meant to lay up treasure for months to come. Late the third evening the boat and barge stopped on its return trip. The boatmen suggested that Gustav go along, as they planned to haul his load the following trip. He hastily climbed on board and got home before breakfast.

But the boat scheduled to pick up Gustav's coal sacks ran aground at the mouth of the river, icebound. In spring break-up the high water claimed it all before the barge could get there. Left without the supplementary fuel they had counted on, the Nyseters asked the Lord to bless their short pile of driftwood. Not surprisingly, from their meager supply they not only kept comfortably warm but also gave away several sledloads to others in need.

"Now I must tell a little about a sled I made even though it wasn't all that great," he wrote home. "Besides our ever-present fuel shortages, I had to have a sled if I wanted to cover any distance at all. It's different here than going out for meetings in Norway. In Alaska most travelers outfit themselves with a dog team. These fine dogs are expensive to buy and costly to feed, so why not hitch myself to a sled? I even experimented with a sail to take advantage of the wind. The boat-sled (unconventional, I'll admit) gave us fun times, a break from the day's routine. Away we flew—Laura as passenger and me as driver—over the flats that lay in front of our house.

"Once spring arrived, I fulfilled my dream of going out on a real evangelistic tour. The expedition proved quite profitable, the natives expressing gratitude for my short visit. They asked if we would consider settling in their village where we could both minister and teach their children.

"Laura and I gave their invitation serious thought, but as we prayed we sensed that the Lord had another plan. He gently reminded us that when we first arrived in the area, we felt temporary—as if still on our way somewhere. Also, we recalled the evening before our leaving Norway the Lord spoke to our hearts about going out like the patriarch Abraham. Without a certain destination, we responded in childlike obedience, taking our days one at a time. We trusted that God would send a man with a message to direct us to a more permanent base when we were ready for it."

A man with a message. They had almost forgotten about him until.... Gustav and Laura had just finished their noon meal when someone knocked at their door.

"Come in."

A stocky-built older man strode in. Who was he? About all they saw at first was his stubby red beard and a quick smile as he began, "God's peace. My name is Høijer. Will you go with me over to Siberia and preach Christ to the Eskimos there?"

His startlingly abrupt introduction sent them momentarily reeling. Regaining their composure, they recalled a previous tug in that westerly direction which had until now seemed nearly impossible. So, with the question put straight to them, they calmly replied, "*Vaersogod* [Be so kind]. Sit down and we'll talk it over."

After a brief discussion of what the man's proposal entailed, the three knelt before the Lord, asking for direction. Soon their guest began praising God for leading him to the right people. They in turn saw before them an up-to-date version of Abraham's servant who had met Rebecca when she went to draw water from the well. They received a clear witness that they should "go with this man" (Gen. 24).

Høijer's boat, the *New York*, lay moored at the dock. Could they leave immediately? With that they balked. Hoijer agreed to wait another twenty-four hours—he could use the time to advantage. While Gustav escorted him to the telegraph station and the post office, Laura started packing. How would they prepare to winter in a remote spot where they couldn't buy even barest necessities?

They were moving to the Diomedes, approximately forty miles west of Cape Prince of Wales, Alaska, and an equal distance from the mainland of Siberia. The eastern island, Little Diomede, with a population of less than one hundred, belongs to the United States; the western island, Big Diomede, with even fewer people, belongs to Russia. Vitus Bering, the Danish navigator sailing under the orders of Peter the Great, discovered them on St. Diomede's Day 1788—hence the name. The inhabitants of these two small rocky islands had close communication and even intermarried, yet they chose to maintain their separate identities.

The thrill of such a move consumed the Nyseters' packing hours. Gradually, however, they had to face the bittersweet consequence of their decision. What about St. Michael? Leaving their new acquaintances wouldn't be easy. As soon as word got around, those whom they called "our flock" hastened over for last visits and heart-touching good-byes. Was it fair to leave without a replacement? Time with them had gone by all too quickly....

"It was on the Fourth of July, 1921, that we arrived in Ketchikan," they reminisced. "Now on the evening of July 4, 1923, Høijer's twelve-meter schooner moved out, taking us away from a place that stands out as an important stepping stone in our lives. The people had grown dear to us.

"We had tried for a year to share the gospel of the Lord Jesus Christ in spite of rather adverse circumstances. Our stay had been a doubleheader. We felt overwhelmed at times by the sin and depression surrounding us and longed to give these dear folk something to hold on to. Nonetheless, we were greenhorns with a lot of Norwegian thought patterns to overcome. Even our concepts of right and wrong were shaded by earlier impressions hardly in keeping with a universal gospel which meets the need of every race. Thus St. Michael had been a school for us, and school days have their own nostalgia. Though we were at peace and happy about moving on, it was also a sad parting.

"What more can we say? Simply this—we have that blessed hope of meeting in heaven those from St. Michael who love our Jesus too. In that eternal home we shall be forever free of this world's encumbrances—sin, weakness of character, cultural differences, sickness and death. Never again to say farewell!"

6

Nils Fredrik Høijer

T his sturdy Swede challenging the Nyseters was born in 1857 in Varmland, Sweden, while northern Europe with its limited resources suffered economically. Families with several children often parceled out offspring to relatives who could feed and clothe them. Young Nils' parents, hoping he would become a state church priest, sent him to live with an uncle who could provide for his education. Being a lad with a mind of his own and certainly not religiously inclined, Nils apprenticed as a village school teacher.

One day a friend persuaded him to go to a Gospel service. The preacher digressed from his message to direct what appears to have been a prophecy straight to the visitor: "You ungodly young man, the God whom we preach is so powerful that He can make you into a servant of His and send you far away to a foreign land where you will proclaim the gospel you now scorn and proclaim it in a language you don't know!"

Some time later Høijer went to another meeting where the minister failed to show up. The small congregation waited. When no one took initiative to begin the service, Høijer, who couldn't stand wasting time, decided somebody ought to do something. Looking around, he spotted a book by the evangelist D.L. Moody. Why not read from that?

"Then," he recounted, "it occurred to me that a proper meeting should open with prayer. That I couldn't do; I wasn't a Christian yet. I asked for someone in the congregation to lead out in prayer before I read one of Moody's sermons. As I stood there reading aloud, the message so gripped me that I decided I must begin a life in fellowship with the Lord. That night I was born again.

"I shared my convictions with some of my comrades who in turn were seized by the same message that changed me. Our pleasurable pursuits turned into prayer meetings. Thus my walk as a missionary began even before I was saved."

In preparation for full-time service, he attended a school of missions in Sweden followed by language training in London. The Swedish Mission Covenant sent him out as their first ordained missionary when he was twenty-three. Though his assignment, working among Swedish seaman, was much appreciated by his countrymen, his efforts away from home were cut short by persecution.

In 1882 the young man went to the Caucasus, a mountainous region occupying the isthmus between the Black and the Caspian seas. He returned to Sweden in the spring of 1883 to marry Anna Dahlman. The couple moved to St. Petersburg where they hoped to establish a missions outreach. Because the Russian government prohibited religious activities, Høijer consolidated his efforts with a Finnish nonalcohol society approved by the proper authorities. Using the society as a shield, he printed gospel literature and worked extensively among the city's prostitutes, roughly estimated at thirty thousand. Many were rescued from lives of utter hopelessness. But again persecution raised its ugly head, this time in the form of a rumor that these converts were being clothed and sold to the Turks. The Høijers were forced to leave.

Their missions headquarters advised Nils and Anna to return to the Caucasus region. After other Swedish workers joined them in 1887, Høijer organized the Evangelistic Armenian Mission Covenant. At their annual meeting two years later, thirteen congregations were represented. Typical of Høijer, he preached an uncompromising salvation message and immediately proceeded to build an indigenous church. As soon as others were qualified to take over his responsibilities, he set off farther afield, often absent for weeks at a stretch from his home base in Tiflis.

On one of his journeys south, he decided to route back through the mountains where the proud freedom-loving Kurds lived. Knowing their reputation for violence, his traveling companions balked. No way would they take the road and by-paths Høijer chose! All right. He'd traverse those mountains by himself.

In keeping with predictions, the loner suddenly found himself surrounded by hateful men. Before they could act, Høijer startled them with a loud command, "Take me to your leader!"

To their leader? Who in the world did this stranger think he was? But the renegades obeyed in spite of themselves. Ushered into the presence of the bandit chief, Hoijer announced in a thunderous voice that echoed through the cave, "I have come as your guest!"

"Where is your weapon?"

"This is my weapon," he said, holding his Bible high. "This is the Highest Spirit's message to mankind."

Overcome by their visitor's command of the situation—or maybe respect for a fellow outlaw—these robbers not only made place for him but also took care of his horse. Following a night of Bible study and visiting in their mountain retreat, several of the renegades escorted him through other dangerous areas so he could continue on his way home.

Before parting, Højer gave them a slip of paper with his name and address. If they would like to know more about the Highest Spirit's message, they could contact him. He would be glad to tell them more.

Months later, a Kurd in full armor with gun and spear knocked at his door. In his hand he held the paper Hoijer had given them. Inviting him in, the missionary led the seeker to a saving knowledge of Jesus Christ. He and Anna kept him in their home a few months while he learned more about the Christian walk. The man returned an on-fire believer to his mountain dwelling. Thus began a breakthrough and subsequent establishment of a solid work in one of the many tribes later discipled by the Covenant people.

Højer dreamed of extending their Russian outreach into China. Without a visa, he left his home in December 1891, showing up several weeks later in East Turkey. Introducing himself to the Russian consulate, he presented copies of a statute passed in 1858 granting freedom to religious endeavors in China. This brave confrontation allowed him to lay groundwork for a congregation in Kashgar, Sin-kiang Province, China. (More than half a century later, word filtered through that the church, going underground, had survived both a Muslim invasion and a Communist purging.)

This journey eventually took Hoijer to Iran where he began yet another work. Johannes Avetaranjanz, an Armenian pastor of many abilities, joined him. When Højer returned to the Caucasus, the Armenian stayed on to do translation work, further strengthening the fledgling church. So began what was often referred to as the world's most outgoing mission among Muslims. The one-of-a-kind evangelist returned to the Caucasus where he hid his efforts behind a storefront, but the business itself didn't do well. Debts piled. How much longer would his supporters stand behind such a venture? On top of these mounting problems, the local authorities began putting pressure on the separatists and shortly thereafter ordered all missionaries out of the country.

Knowing that one of the leaders of the young church would be exiled to Siberia and almost certain death, Høijer helped him out by giving up his place on their family visa. The man traveled with courageous Anna and their two-year-old son, Walter. As a couple they slipped quite easily through controls with the little boy on the man's arm, patting him on the cheek and calling him "Papa."

The real Høijer? He showed up weeks later after traveling hundreds of miles (a distance equal to that between Rome and Stockholm) alone. Riding his horse at night, resting in haystacks or whatever hiding place he could find by day, he finally reached Plot in the Ukraine. There he sold his horse and completed the journey on foot.

The missionary seemed to have a knack for finding individuals to be rescued. On another occasion he saved a young teacher from banishment by smuggling her into Sweden as his companion—an act that raised not a few eyebrows.

When confronted on what was narrowly viewed as questionable behavior, he addressed his accuser. "What if it were your wife who for the name of Jesus was being doomed to Siberian exile? If I had risked my life to take her with me across the Caucasus mountains, over the Caspian Sea and through Russia all the way home to Sweden and to you, would you have thanked me?"

It appeared, however, that the doors to his beloved Russia were definitely closing. Though Høijer tried to content himself with living in Sweden, a missions call burned in his heart night and day. In 1903, he and eight other workers formed what is now known as the Slavic Missions Society for the spread of the gospel in east European countries. He visited Russia once more, but only briefly, before traveling to America to raise funds for spreading the gospel in those hard-pressed lands.

Unfortunately, the crusader's trips back to Sweden became less frequent. Local legend relayed that on one of his visits no one stepped forward to meet the stranger coming up the path. Not until the family's dog rose from his place, slowly wagging his tail in recognition, did they realize that it was Nils who had come home. No, he couldn't stay long. He had so much to do....

This one-of-a-kind missionary who burned with a love for Russia nurtured a hope that Alaska would provide a back door into the chambers of its far east. Thus, propelled by a vision and a sense of urgency no one else could fully understand, he contacted the Nyseters.

7

Predecessors

G ustav gave a thumbnail sketch of Høijer's two years before their encounter at St. Michael. The veteran, now past age sixty and often referred to respectfully as Old Høijer, burned with one desire. He must find the elusive door into Russia—if indeed there was one. Upon persuading Covenant missionary Evald Ost to help him, they borrowed a single-mast sloop, *Jenny*, to take them across the Bering Strait to check out possibilities for evangelism.

Høijer approached the commissars in charge and, encouraged by their cordiality, began laying plans bigger than he could handle alone. If only Brother Ost, a born navigator, would team up with them on a more permanent basis.... Ost, however, would not be persuaded; he had his work already laid out for him.

Though disappointed, Høijer remained undaunted. The following year he bought a wreck of a boat, the *New York*, in Nome. With an eye for detail, he carefully outfitted it for plying the often-stormy waters of his proposed missionary journeys. He also selected native helpers: Harry Soxie (an interpreter) and family, George Taruk (captain), and a boatman. A young Swedish seminary graduate and his American bride also traveled with them.

The team of ten sailed across the Bering Strait, arriving at Little Diomede mid-October. Inasmuch as the island had been without a teacher for several years, the American authorities readily gave permission for them to occupy the schoolhouse. After unloading his passengers with their personal effects, Høijer planned to sail back to Nome for food and fuel to last the winter. On departure day the weather appeared favorable enough, but the captain had barely weighed anchor and started the engine when it suddenly stalled. Then the open sea, unable to resist a few season's-end punches against Little Diomede's unprotected coastline, sent a huge breaker that tossed the helpless craft toward the beach.

One of Diomede's medicine men, Azzakazik, quickly secured a rope to the top of the mast and with remarkable dexterity swung himself on board. He carefully maneuvered the vessel toward land—and in such a way that the waves would be less likely to damage it. Later everyone put shoulders to the task of dragging the boat up on solid ground just as pack ice closed in behind them.

The little colony in the schoolhouse put in a rugged winter, using from their food store sparingly lest rations would run out before spring. Their pitiful fuel supply wouldn't so much as warm the main room enough for them to hold school as planned. Feeling sorry for this overgrown family, the natives helped out of their penury as much as they could. Only one commodity had they to spare—time. An excerpt from Høijer's daybook gives interesting insight as to how he applied his hours: "Harry preached as usual in the meeting. It was the first Sunday that we were able to use Scripture translated into Yupik text. I managed to put together an alphabet of Latin, Russian, and Armenian letters, blending the Russian *sch* sound with two or three Armenian sounds...." Leave it to Høijer, a man credited with having mastered no less than fourteen languages.

Eight months later spring broke winter's silence, setting the captives free to sail eastward. To assure themselves a home base on free soil, the Soxie family was elected to remain at Little Diomede. On June 11th the *New York* set sail for East Cape.

In spite of annoying encounters with drift ice, they crossed the other half of the Bering Strait without incident, casting anchor outside the village of Nuokan, the farthest west point of Siberia. The three Swedish workers went ashore to a house where two government employees lived. The employee who spoke English fairly well bade them welcome, expressing pleasure that anyone would visit that lonely spot on such an errand as theirs. Nevertheless, it lay outside his jurisdiction to give them permission to stay. They must inquire of higher authorities stationed in Ualen on the north side of the peninsula.

While Høijer went by dog team to the designated headquarters, the young couple bided their time in the house with the two Russian men. Whether the one who didn't understand much English knew what the visit was about remains debatable. Perhaps watching his comrade in pleasant conversation and preparing a meal for the foreigners made him jealous or suspicious. Whatever, he only looked on narrowly—apparently waiting his chance. When the friendly Russian stood to go into the next room, the disgruntled one leveled the barrel of his gun and fired. The bullet went through his victim's head, through the wall, and outdoors!

The Swedish couple stared in horror as blood splattered on the woman's parka. Fleeing from the house and down to the beach, they rowed back to the mission boat, climbed aboard, and hid.

When Høijer returned in triumph with his desired permit, he met with sorry news. The seriousness of the situation demanded that they leave immediately. Reluctantly Høijer gave orders to sail back to Diomede, then to the mainland. As for the terrified workers, they had had enough of Siberia already. Nor would they ever return!

The old soldier of the Cross later described arriving in Nome with his retreating workers as the heaviest day of his life. His plans for Siberian missions lay in ruins.

At that low point someone who had heard about Gustav and Laura suggested he contact them. Grasping at a straw, the loner sailed the long distance around Norton Sound to St. Michael. By the time he reached the Nyseters' door, however, he began entertaining second thoughts about his impulsive action. What goes with this couple whom everyone in town seemed to know? If they were so accepted, would they consider uprooting and going where they might have to face rejection? In all honesty he couldn't paint them a promising picture.

Little wonder that Old Høijer rejoiced when he received their "Ya!"

8

Arrived!

=◆=

The Nyseters strained for one last glimpse of St. Michael doing its best to celebrate Independence Day. Round the bend they switched interest to the small boat with the name of America's biggest city proudly carrying them over the waves in a northerly direction. Even Laura, who could get sick at the sight of a boat, admitted that it rode the waves well.

At last on their way, Høijer appeared less pressured. Once they stopped at a small rocky island to gather bird eggs to supplement rations on board. By six o'clock the following morning they had arrived in Unalakleet where the Swedish Covenant Mission had built up a solid work over a period of years.

While enjoying a hearty breakfast, Høijer basked in the company of old friends who saw in him a replica of Unalakleet's first missionary, Axel Karlson. He likewise had engaged in gospel work in the Caucasus region of Russia before being banished to Siberia. When Sweden's king successfully pressured the Czar to release Swedish subjects,

Karlson emigrated to San Francisco. In 1887, after a year learning English, he boarded ship for Alaska.

In St. Michael, Karlson met Nashalook, an outstanding leader among his own people. Inasmuch as both men spoke Russian and English fluently, they made a quick breakthrough from acquaintance to friendship. Nashalook invited Karlson to his home in Unalakleet, but as could be expected, not all the local residents welcomed this stranger. The clever Nashalook took care of that by conveniently placing him under house arrest until tempers cooled. Three months later Karlson came out of hiding, but still under the headman's protection. When one of the local fellows, influenced by a shaman, raised an ax above Karlson's head, the strong arm of Nashalook's brother deflected the intended blow.

An entry in the missionary's journal gave a brief description of the village: "All the living are underground; the dead lay on top." Wanting a breath of fresh air for his church and school, Karlson put up a log building that stood two-thirds higher than any of the surrounding dwellings. Turnabout. The living on top!

Karlson's wife, Hanna, joined him and kept home fires burning while he dogteamed to surrounding settlements, thus paving the way for later workers with medical and teaching skills. Belonging to a generation that equated hard work with survival and their own self-respect, they came with a Bible in one hand, a tool in the other. Building homes and planting gardens, Unalakleet began its own climb to be one of the most progressive villages of the north.

While the Swedes reminisced, Gustav and Laura got acquainted with people whose lives would be touching theirs through years to come. Several hours later, after taking on another passenger, the boat lifted anchor once more. On shore most of Unalakleet's population had gathered to say good-bye to the travelers by singing, "What a day that will be when we meet on heaven's shore," in both Eskimo and English. The Scandinavians resounded in their respective languages. Then, on both land and aboard ship, believers knelt together to pray God's protection over those who went and those who stayed.

After a few hours on a rolling sea that made several of them "green behind the gills," they came to Shaktoolik. Seeing their frustrating attempts to enter the shallow river, local men came out and guided them through a channel deep enough to keep the *New York* afloat.

How quickly one forgets the discomforts of travel once he puts his feet on firm ground! The friendly natives, many of whom were radiant Christians, welcomed them. The day's celebration should begin with a meeting. While someone scrounged gas boxes (used for shipping cans of appliance gas) for seating in a large tent, another rang the bell by beating on an empty five-gallon gas can. One hundred percent turnout. Afterward, dipping into kettles of steaming reindeer meat, they told about their earlier years of persistent poverty. In answer to prayer, the Lord sent wild game their way and helped them find ocean fish in abundance. Now they ate the good of the land.

That evening a thoughtful couple offered the Nyseters their bed complete with mosquito netting. They hadn't complained about accommodations on the *New York,* but what a contrast! The next morning the village insisted on yet another meeting for the benefit of latecomers from outlying camps.

"Wonderful meeting, wonderful place," Nyseter wrote in his letter home. "Shaktoolik with its Siberian poppies and other wild flowers seemed to exude a healing balm that will linger with us for days."

They journeyed on past fields decorated with domesticated reindeer. The original herds imported from Siberia and Lapland had been accompanied by seasoned herders able to teach local Eskimos their skill. Although not as successful as had been hoped, the enterprise nonetheless kept villages from starving and played a continuing role in the local economy.

The travelers stayed overnight in a lagoon, a rhythmic slapping of gentle waves against the hull of the *New York* lulling them to sleep. The following morning they arrived at Elim where missionary Evald Ost and his family welcomed them. Ost, a Swedish immigrant, had come to Alaska with his bride, Ruth, in 1910. Besides their own eight children, they made room for an average of eighteen to twenty needy native youngsters as part of their extended family. Not always in the best of health, Ruth nevertheless filled her multiple roles cheerfully and capably: school teacher, musician, Sunday school director, postmistress, and midwife. Folk knew her best, however, as a gentle women whose home became a sanctuary for the lonely, the disappointed, those in want of healing for their wounded spirits.

Elim, named for an oasis where the Hebrew people camped, was almost an oasis in itself—quiet, sheltered, and with trees and bushes growing all the way down to the beach. Gustav became ecstatic, "Look, Laura. It's like a real forest. Norway's Østerdalen again!"

The Nyseters absorbed every minute to its fullest, not expecting another Sunday like it for a long time to come. On Diomede they wouldn't be immediately surrounded by those of like faith.

The next day the *New York* resumed its course with more passengers, Ruth Ost and four of her children, who were going as far as Nome. All went well until, rounding a spit, a contrary wind forced them to seek shelter up a small river. After gathering driftwood and warming themselves by a roaring bonfire, part of the travelers chose to relieve their cramped sleeping quarters by stretching out right there.

Høijer felt it safe to start out again the following day, but again winds decreed otherwise. They barely made it beyond the spit and up the other side when they spotted just a short distance from shore a large house with reindeer grazing nearby. Seeing no herders of whom they could ask permission, they upheld the unwritten law of the trail: Use what you need, with consideration for the owner and the needs of others who might come behind you.

After about twenty-four hours, the capricious wind had shifted, making the *New York* no longer safe where Høijer had secured it. On their way again! Just as everyone got on board, the boat suddenly heaved toward land. Over went the kitchen box. Their precious cast iron skillet and faithful old coffeepot sank to the bottom of the river. The incident, amounting to a near catastrophe, ended in laughs as one of the men hung over the side of the boat to fish for lost treasure. Hooray! Got it all! Once more Høijer ordered his crew to lift anchor.

They started the engine. It quit. Within minutes huge waves carried the helpless craft toward the beach for a pounding where it would have shipwrecked had the men not fought with poles and oars to keep it afloat. At last they were able to hoist the sail and restart the engine. They moved out, but the women on board didn't take the heavy swells with comfort. So Gustav was appointed cook.

Laura's side-glance meant, "Here comes another catastrophe." Gustav quipped, "It's all right. Not many are hungry anyway."

The more recent passengers got off at Nome where the Nyseters met the couple who had the dreadful experience on the Siberian coast. Still feeling crushed, they were waiting for travel connections stateside and possibly to Sweden. With no reason to take their arctic outfits home—and maybe the reminders hurt—they gave them to the Nyseters. And their gifts came as an answer to prayer. Gustav recalled wanting to buy a parka for Laura in St. Michael, but she had shrugged her shoulder with, "Let's forget it. The Lord has promised me a fur parka—and it will be a pretty one too."

Saturday Høijer changed their course to northeast, following the coastline until they reached Teller, where they veered west and anchored off a sand spit. To keep the Lord's Day, Høijer suggested they all go ashore to relax. Gustav and Laura, realizing that soon their fifteen years of longing would be fulfilled, only rested outwardly. Inside they were jumping up and down.

Midnight plus one minute—Monday—still daylight and driftwood everywhere begging to be picked up. Eagerly they all pitched in, filling every available space in the boat with wood. Living on Diomede required fuel even in midsummer. Setting out again, they sailed for hours along a barren coastline, eyes straining for distant scenes. Long before they reached the most westerly point of Alaska, Taruk pointed out landmarks—the Diomedes and East Cape on the Asian side. At the foot of a vast ice field lay Nuokan, a large Eskimo village. Although at least seventy miles away, the clear morning air brought it into sharp focus.

"Hallelujah! Thank you, Lord!" What else could they say? No longer a dream or vision, but reality. The ends of the earth.

One more stop, Cape Prince of Wales. Wars were common in the old days when the Siberians came to the Alaska side in their skin boats to rob and plunder. On the high cliffs just behind the village stands a row of stones that could easily be mistaken for people—set there to trick those Asian "Vikings" into thinking scouts stood continually on watch. "Or at least," their informant quickly added, "so the story goes."

Having to anchor the New York far out, only Høijer and two of the crew rowed ashore. Then it began to rain, enveloping the coast in dense fog. Nonetheless, they soon returned with supplies, hoisted the dory back on deck and proceeded westward. Visibility amounted to only a few boat lengths ahead, the island concealed in a mist. How to know when they got there?

As they moved next to, almost under, the whitened cliffs of Diomede, feathered parents flew about in a panic for fear someone might disturb their babies. Their shrieks, dependable as a whistle buoy, indicated that the boat was right on target.

Taruk at the wheel swung around the southern tip of the island and up the east side. A subdued sea, not in the mood to fight just then, let them anchor near the village situated on a point sloping toward the water. When in direct line with the schoolhouse, the Nyseters saw the community come alive at once. Men hurriedly jumped into their skin boats, headed out to meet them, and climbed aboard. The crew, one of whom was a Diomeder, and passengers all received the same glad welcome.

Rain bucketing down dampened no one's spirit; Diomeders pitched in to help transport baggage and supplies of immediate use. Not knowing what to do, Gustav and Laura stood to one side on the rocky shore, basking in the thrill of having reached their goal—for whatever that meant or whatever it might bring.

9

Roots Down

===◆===

Høijer had arranged for the newcomers to live in the schoolhouse with the understanding they pick up the work that had failed the previous winter. Well after midnight, the last villager went home, leaving Høijer and the newcomers to themselves. Then more talk until they could unwind enough to think about sleep.... But first, time on their knees before God.

During this short devotion, Laura sensed a definite word being spoken to her heart: "O Lord, my strength, and my fortress, and my refuge in the day of affliction, the Gentiles shall come unto thee from the ends of the earth, and shall say, Surely our fathers have inherited lies, vanity, and things wherein there is no profit" (Jer. 16:19). Accepting it as a promise to grasp when the going got rough, they made a note in their Bibles so they wouldn't forget....

The next day everyone scurried around like squirrels getting ready for winter. In the evening Høijer called a meeting, obviously enjoying his role of speaking to the islanders who listened attentively. Later that night he and his crew boarded the mission boat for East Cape, which lay about four hours away. The weather and Russian authorities together spelled uncertainty. Old Høijer's most sincere, "I'll be right back," meant little.

No matter how much the Nyseters appreciated their friend, they were glad to be at home alone. The sea journey with its close quarters had afforded more togetherness than they had really wanted. Ah, time to stretch out and enjoy each other and neighbors close by. This was living! After a couple days, however, they concurred that a perfect balance wasn't easily achieved. Children came in and out quite freely. Adults visited on a more regular basis, often bringing gifts like edible greens, small razorbill birds and seal liver (a real delicacy). The Nyseters gave from their store, apparently without either side feeling obligated. Through give and take they were learning each other's expectations.

Communication consisted mostly of imprompt sign language. Gustav shook his head, "They're eager to teach us words, but we seem slow catching on. I don't know if the fault lies with the teachers, the students, the language it-self, or a combination of all three."

Drawing a crowd for a meeting, however, came easy. Upon hearing the bell, folk streamed in. Besides the warmth of singing along with them, the Nyseters were responding to the heartbeat of the village. Other than music, they had little to give. Nonetheless, they were laying a foundation against the day when their ears would begin to pick up Eskimo words.

"Laura," Gustav commented one evening, "have you noticed how nice looking these people are? If they experienced salvation and spruced up a bit, this could be an up-and-coming community." He paused. "But we must be careful. We didn't come to carve out another little Norway."

Though the Nyseters were proud of their heritage, they didn't try to deny its tarnished past. The Romans had classed the Scandinavians as rank barbarians, and with good reason. Even after being introduced to Christianity, warring Vikings weren't exactly sainted overnight. So, by comparison, North American natives didn't look the worst.

Gustav, an avid reader and no less a writer, had limited opportunity to pursue either seriously, so he poured himself into detailed accounts of everyday living. With good-byes to outgoing missionaries carrying the distinct probability of a final farewell, he knew their letters home would be read and reread before being laid away in a trunk. Gustav described the village as he and Laura saw it:

"Let's pretend we're going visiting. Walking along we come to a raised mound with a lighted square in the middle of it. When voices drift up from beneath, we realize we're standing on the roof of a house. The light spot is a gut-skin window in the center, which serves its purpose remarkably well, admitting light while being opaque enough to keep the curious from peeking in.

"Walking around to the lower side of the house, we find an entrance marked by what looks like an unusual rock formation on its low roof. On closer examination we discover it's the shoulder blade of a whale, about three feet across its widest part. Irregular stone work forms the base of this tunnel-like windbreak, so small we must get down and crawl.

"Half crouched, we cross the threshold into a driftwood lean-to that looks two-storied, but is hardly high enough for a grown person to stand upright. We shuffle past all sorts of stuff, careful not to step on sleepy-eyed dogs curled up against each other to keep warm. A low "loft" provides storage space for tools, food, and clothing that can tolerate dampness. We knock (a formality reserved for outsiders). Someone answers, 'Come.'

"We get down on all fours again to crawl through the opening that serves as a doorway. (Now I know for sure what the Bible means when it speaks of the strait and narrow way!) To open the 'door,' I lift a gunnysack hanging there. I go in first so I can turn around and lend a hand to the next person. I've had practice as my wife needs help when she wears too much bulky clothing. A tug and a pull, a bit of humor, and we're in.

"Asked to sit down, we seat ourselves on the floor just as the others are doing, tucking our legs under us to save space. The clean wood floor, well polished by the seat of our pants, becomes dining table, chair, and bed all in one. A meat-cutting board too, for scooped out in one of the heavy boards is a shallow bowl to lay the head of a seal when skinning and flaying it. 'Practical people,' we whisper in quiet admiration.

"'Amazing that it can be so light in here with that kind of windowpane,' you might add.

"Yes, but wait until it is layered with frost as thick as your thumb or covered over with snow. A strain on the eyes at mid-day! The room measures about ten feet square— an average size house. Along the walls the room is about three feet high, but in the center a man my height can stand upright. The wall planks made of hand-hewn driftwood stand on end; near the ceiling hangs a rack for drying clothes and skins. Only the largest homes have a heavier frame that serves as a bed.

"A layer of earth between the outer stone and inner walls serves as insulation, keeping the place draft-free even during the meanest winter blizzard. Light is provided by a primitive oil lamp that looks like the oven door of a small cookstove placed on wooden legs. This 'door' holds seal or walrus oil, with dried pulverized swamp moss strewn in one corner as a wick. A pair of iron sticks is used to spread the flame until the lamp burns evenly over its entire surface. The lamp also gives out heat enough for frying meat or for cooking in a heavy pot suspended over it.

"The average home boasts little else. The family gets by with some cups, bowls, a teakettle, and other cooking utensils stacked in the corner. Only the more prosperous would have an alarm clock, a chest or cupboard to hold miscellaneous items, and perhaps a portable sewing machine.

"The people are usually adequately clothed. When in the house they leave their footwear near the door and hang heavy outer parkas on pegs. I have happened upon men and women sitting without anything on their upper bodies, but they didn't pretend modesty for my sake. These habits, however, may not be a part of Eskimo culture as a whole.

"We're invited to share a meal. The housewife serves cooked seal or walrus meat on a tray about 28 inches long and almost as wide. Her knife, called an *ulu*, is pie-shaped with a small handle at the point, which fits into the palm of the hand so pressure can be applied easily. She might also bring on a cup of oil or a dish of greens that have been soaked in fat.

"After I return thanks, we begin—each helping himself as quickly as possible. The head of the house picks up his big work knife and hacks off a long strip from the thighbone. Holding the meat between his teeth, he cuts it with his knife. When I first saw this, I worried about his nose and mouth with a weapon so close. No danger. He knows what he's doing.

"These people have their etiquette too. With four fingers (little finger excluded) each one grasps a piece of meat, dips it in oil, and quickly shoves it into his mouth before the oil drips off. Careful as we are, our fingers become greasy—oil shines around the mouth too. So the hostess hands us a wet rag that we pass from one to the other. Now the next course.

"After the wife clears the table, she serves tea with sugar, if we wish. She also sets out a kind of cake made from flour, water, and a pinch of soda stirred together and browned in seal oil. For us who aren't used to seal oil, the cake isn't the best. The Eskimos, however, like it—maybe an acquired taste as a tiny bit of seal fat is placed on a baby's tongue right after he is born. Getting ready to leave, we say a hearty 'Echlaganame [Thank you].'

"Our hostess explains without apology that she would have done better by us if the weather hadn't been so warm. In winter she can make us some Eskimo ice cream, a combination of reindeer tallow and snow. Besides that, she has another specialty. Her recipe: a walrus head laying indoors a week or so until it is well soured. Then she sets it out to freeze, bringing it in later to serve as a frozen delicacy.

"With a 'Good-bye, so long,' we crawl through the passageway again, out where we breathe deeply of fresh air. After sitting in close quarters with our warm clothing on and drinking hot tea, there's nothing like a north wind to slap us wide-awake again.

"Noticing a dog sniffing greedily at a whale bone laying just outside the door, we lift one edge of it cautiously. Ah, that's what he's after! The flat bone covers the entrance to a cellar heaped with chunks of walrus meat, much of which is covered with green mold. Believe me, a whiff of that makes us drop the door in a hurry. In all fairness we hasten to clarify their diet. If our good neighbors didn't balance it with sour meat, feasting on fresh birds in the spring would be more than their systems could tolerate. Aware of this, they plan their food supply accordingly.

"I still say, let the Eskimos be themselves. Only let them know freedom from bondage through the atoning work of Jesus Christ and all else will fall into place for their good."

10

First Weeks

E arly twentieth-century immigrants could hardly be called spendthrifts. It cost a hard-earned penny to cross the Atlantic and begin life anew. A winter in St. Michael made the Nyseters still more frugal, careful not only with what money can buy but also with that which cost effort.

The simple act of fetching water on Little Diomede was a hassle. They climbed over boulders to get to a stream on the other side of the village, then sloshed much of the precious water climbing over the same boulders coming back. If only the source were close at hand....

"Laura, look!" Gustav sounded as excited as a sailor adrift who had finally spotted land. While setting the supply room in order, he discovered a sink and a water tank of several thousand liters along with pipes that apparently hadn't been connected in years. Among his own things he came up with an old faucet that he had packed along on a hunch that he just might be needing it. Sure enough!

Before long, all the villagers could draw water at the schoolhouse. Never mind that the water came out brown— it would clear up after the pipes had been used more. Strange...no matter how much they drew, it still came out badly discolored. Worse yet, a green scum developed on top. What in the world? Then they saw it—droppings from thousands of birds circling overhead. Gustav improvised a cover for the tank right away!

While Laura scrubbed and cleaned, Gustav built a small planter against the side of the schoolhouse. Carefully he set out the few scrawny cabbage starts he had brought from St. Michael. July 21st—and so cold that he had to wear gloves. As anyone might have guessed, the whole gardening bit became a joke. "I can't help it," he half apologized. "I know that every year I'll go through this. I have to because I'm still a farmer at heart."

The man's better judgment overruled, persuading him to find out what the island itself had to offer. One day a neighbor showed him how to dig Eskimo potatoes, nodules hardly bigger than his fingertips, which grew in damp, almost swampy, soil. Simmered in fat, their sweet taste provided a pleasant variation to usual island fare, especially after months without fresh vegetables. If a person were lucky, he could get several pounds in a day. However, they seemed hardly worth the effort considering the time it took to clean them.

Gustav also tried his hand at catching birds for the stew pot. Throwing a long-handled sling to bring down birds in flight required both skill and strength. He finally mastered an art that never really appealed to him, so he came home with only enough to satisfy their immediate need.

Gustav did go on an exciting walrus hunt, but again the gentle man couldn't quite get into the swing of it. His description revealed a certain reluctance: "I've stood on shore and heard the din of ten or twenty rifles at once, all aimed at a single target. Unfair as it was, I watched the giant creature dive below the surface of the water—only to resurface as victor a long way off. Nevertheless, if asked to give my opinion on the future of this great animal, I would be compelled to say that we had best be wary of hunting fever. Handled unwisely, it contributes more to our loss than to our gain."

The couple chose to enjoy the outdoors in other ways. On one of the first clear days making it possible, they climbed up the steep rocky incline to the summit about fifteen hundred feet above sea level. What a view! On the Alaska side one snow-covered peak after another rose as far as eye could see. In the opposite direction stretched Siberia's mountain ranges and unending moors. Big Diomede, the last Asian outpost, they had seen from their own door. Now, looking down from this vantagepoint, the short span between seemed to shrink into only a few hundred feet.

That deception stayed with them. Later, hearing that Big Diomede abounded in driftwood, they decided to go there in the mission schooner's old flat-bottom rowboat, which Gustav had already proven seaworthy. When the right kind of weather smiled on them, rowing to the neighboring island would be like crossing a narrow fjord back home. Not only were they almost sure to find wood, but it would be fun to set foot on Russian soil—over the international date line, where man has said that week days begin and end. The Big Diomeders had Sunday while the Little Diomeders were still having Saturday, a fact the islanders themselves chose to disregard. How could one be so arrogant as to think himself a day ahead of his neighbors?

The morning dawned bright and clear. Presuming their sister island lay only a stone's toss away, the Nyseters set out for a leisurely tour. Oh? They had failed to reckon with the current's strong northerly pull. Gustav had to set the bow in a southwesterly direction in order to continue their course straight west. To their alarm, that narrow strip of water seemed to widen while they rowed. As they neared the island, heavy swells prevented their landing. After they finally managed to turn around, the current carried them northward. Enveloped by a dense, soupy fog, they would be lost at sea unless the Lord intervened.

Finally they heard the pounding of breakers against the cliffs of their island. Never had the surf sounded so good! Gustav put all his strength to the oars until they were in safe proximity of their own shores, which he hugged close as he dared. At last, the schoolhouse was in sight! Numbed from cold and tense hours seated in a little rowboat, Gustav and Laura woodenly forced themselves out, then pulled the boat well above reach of an incoming tide.

The couple felt thankful and, at the same time, sheepish. Their stupidity! Had a grain of pride lured them out on their own without asking advice from the locals? The village men knew what had happened of course, but that was all right too. Like anyone else, the missionaries had to admit their folly. And, blessed thought, God isn't in a hurry to pull guardian angels off duty when we fail to use the good sense He gave us.

The lesson learned didn't mean that the wood on Big Diomede lay forgotten. Gustav and Laura set out again on a day with a cooperating wind holding them even with the current. They pulled the boat up on the west side of the island, then scrambled higher to sure footing. There they stumbled across an abandoned village below which ran a creek with an abundance of driftwood left by incoming tides. Eagerly they started gathering, then suddenly stopped. Think! They would have to lug it about five miles to the most northerly point of the island before rowing back home. They sighed. So much for that bright idea, but it had given them a delightful outing before winter set in anyway.

Two days later the *New York* appeared, not from the west as expected but from the east, rounding the southern tip of the island as it had when they had come from Alaska. Where had Høijer been?

The veteran described tightening Soviet control. In spite of the natives' wishes and his being handed a permit only weeks before, the authorities denied him the right to establish a mission. He pressed his cause until they agreed to his settling as a private citizen. Underneath, of course, he hoped to stay a winter with an interpreter and secretly work at translating the Bible.

On their return, the captain happened to chart their course too far south. Missing Little Diomede entirely, they decided to sail to the mainland for more supplies. What was that about coming right back? Never mind, he did what he could. Now, would Gustav go with them to East Cape, stopping at Big Diomede to pick up the wood he and Laura had gathered two days previous? They needed a full load if he and his interpreter were to winter in Siberia.

Thus it came about that a few hours later Gustav got his first glimpse of Nuokan. While the natives came out in their umiaks to transport supplies from their vessel at anchor, Gustav looked on. He saw little else than a few unpretentious buildings. One scene, however, stamped itself indelibly on his mind. On shore stood at least fifty children who, unless someone reached them, would grow up in the heathen darkness of their forefathers.

By nine o'clock in the evening the *New York* set its course eastward again, but heavy fog hindered their stopping at Big Diomede. "Thank God we couldn't," Gustav said afterwards. "We found out we would have put some lives in jeopardy. A little settlement not far from that neat wood supply counted on it to see them through the winter."

The mission boat managed one more trip to Alaska's mainland to pick up a full load of fuel without depleting someone else's wood box.

"All right, winter, we're ready for you!" Gustav shouted lightheartedly. Not quite ready, of course, yet they were far enough ahead that he could meet the coming season with a twinge of excitement.

"It's something of a thrill to see the ocean throw a fit of temper when one sits comfortably indoors looking out," Gustav wrote. "But when for eight or ten days on end a storm howls with sea foaming and ghostly fog banks sweep eerily by, the pleasure wears thin. The big schoolhouse lies so close to the sea that when waves dashed their highest they came within five or six meters of us—and covered our windows with salt. Ships couldn't come near our island during storms, and those finding refuge beneath Big Diomede didn't exactly lay in snug harbor either.

"When nature's temper tantrum is over, we may waken to a quiet sunny morning. That usually meant caravans of half a dozen skin boats coming at once from maritime Siberia. Figuring ten persons to an umiak, it's easy to see how we overflowed with guests. A number of women would come too, though always in the minority."

Such a get-together meant greeting old friends, upholding traditions and peaceable relations between two worlds. Then there was the commercial side—here they might be able to get "white man's food" unavailable on their shores. Bartering could go on for days and, if they were lucky, a storm might afford an excuse to linger longer. Older men who had learned a smattering of English when whalers plied their coast retrieved half-forgotten words to beg for first one thing and then another. Too, they wanted to greet these foreigners, observe their different ways....

"I haven't coveted the title," Gustav wrote, "but I think some were curious—wanting to find out if I was a medicine man of reputation. First came a young fellow with a swollen finger. If I could heal it, then I wasn't the worst. I tried to tell my patient that we believed in an unseen being whom we call God. He has a Son named Jesus who died for our sins as well as for our physical needs. When we pray to Him, He helps us in our weakness; He cares about our hurts. At the same time we have to keep ourselves clean so wounds can heal naturally.

"I washed the infected finger with boric acid solution and bandaged it. Then I knelt and prayed for both body and soul. Poor folk, like sheep without a shepherd. We're beginning to understand more clearly the word the Lord gave us when we left Norway: 'There lives a folk in misery and darkness. Those people I love. To fulfill my word that the gospel shall go out to the ends of the earth, I send you.'

"Oh that we carry out our divine commission and bring light to those who sit in darkness! So what if we sometimes got weary entertaining this flock of visitors? We're being granted the unique opportunity of sowing the seed of the gospel among people who come from the other side of the strait. If we can't go to them, they can come to us. We count further on the power of God's Word that He said will not return to Him without accomplishing His purpose."

When their visitors left, the couple turned again to preparing for winter. Once Gustav and Laura traveled almost effortlessly by rowboat southward along the coast, propelled by a moderately strong wind. They went ashore to gather berries and greens for canning, but the wind picked up before they began their return. Hard as he rowed, Gustav couldn't buck the tide. At last they had to drag the little boat up on land and make the arduous trek home afoot. As for the boat, some sneaking waves came and whisked it away.

Gustav shrugged off the incident. "Sometimes we win and sometimes we lose. I made up for it later by repairing another boat for Høijer. Besides, if that's the worst loss my wife and I have to face here at the earth's farthest ends, we'll be getting by easy."

11

Maritime Siberia

A stormy day in September, the *New York* appeared near the other island, seeking refuge from a raging tempest. Four days later the water calmed enough for it to come limping over, rudder broken, mast uprooted, one anchor lost and another anchor rope worn nearly in two. No food or matches on board. The Nyseters quickly ushered the bedraggled crew into the schoolhouse to stay while the men frantically repaired the battered vessel.

Though winter sent its calling card (snow on top of Big Diomede) early, Høijer insisted on leaving for East Cape as soon as possible. He must deliver material salvaged from an abandoned house on the Alaska side. He asked (or commanded?), "Gustav, you will go to help build?"

Within a couple of hours the mission schooner sailed westward, leaving Laura alone on Little Diomede. Eight hours later the *New York* arrived at Ualen, about ten miles from Nuokan, where they planned to settle. Høijer had to clear customs and get permission for Gustav to remain as his employee. Paperwork would be slow because a steamboat from Vladivostok—probably the only one of the year—had also arrived.

Gustav and his interpreter, Harry Soxie, stayed on board watching Høijer go over to the steamer, where he hoped to buy coal. Then the wind picked up with such force that those left behind didn't dare row the fifty yards to shore. Laying at anchor almost forty-eight hours, they could only wonder about the man whom Gustav dubbed a "Swedish original." Had he gotten arrested or what? Though customarily steady as Gibraltar, Gustav fought a queasy stomach and the wildest of imaginations. Recalling what had happened to his predecessors didn't help! After getting used to the rolling sea and forcing himself to eat, he decided to face their situation more realistically: when weather cleared, he and Harry would find Høijer...rescue him...do something.

Finally going ashore, the two men made their way into dwellings quite different from those on Little Diomede. They looked like anthills with the lower part built of stone and sod, the upper framework draped with walrus hides. Gloomy interiors allowed only faint streaks of daylight to seep through holes and cracks. In the center of the main room, upon a platform about eighteen inches higher than the floor, stood a box-like tent with a flat roof.

After entering a number of these dwellings, the pair poked their way farther in by lifting a corner of the central tent. Talk about nerve, but they were nearly frantic to find their missing man! Several times they intruded upon women and children sitting on the floor naked, warming themselves by an oil lamp. Gustav confessed it was the first time in his life that for shyness he couldn't look directly at the opposite sex, though he was sure they had on the clothes they were born with—a weak stab at humor, perhaps a cover-up for feeling guilty about having invaded their privacy. He sensed their embarrassment that a total stranger had seen them unclothed, but he didn't know how to apologize. Besides, he wasn't trying to look at or even think about them. He wanted Høijer!

At last the two men entered the home of a highly respected herder, where they sat on a low bench in front of the inner room. When made aware of their presence, the man promptly ordered someone to lay a reindeer skin on the bench for them—a kindly gesture. Harry managed to communicate a little with this family of a kindred race known as Chuckchee, who spoke neither English nor Eskimo. Høijer's whereabouts? Not a clue.

"You might know," Gustav blurted out, "that when we were sure of the worst, we found the old Swede. What were we worried about? He'd been living quite comfortably with the Russian officers who had arranged a feast for him and other invited guests."

Gustav wanted to give him a piece of his mind (in Scandinavian, of course) but was too relieved to remain angry. Furthermore, he felt refreshed to see among the Soviets free-thinking men unafraid to be themselves. Hoijer, Gustav, and Harry were treated most courteously, even to drinking coffee with the governor in his state house. The crew also was allowed ashore. Although everyone spoke English as a second language, conversation flowed freely. Sensing approval by the authorities, the newcomers rowed back to the ship with high hopes for the months ahead.

They waited out another storm before finally arriving in Nuokan. The natives rallied as one, dragging out two big umiaks with which to transport building material and supplies. Hoijer rented a small frame house that had belonged to the headman's son who had been lost at sea. According to an old belief, his spirit still lived there, so it couldn't be sold.

Høijer gave Gustav basic instructions: winterize the house, hire a crew to help with the heavy work and a servant to spare him hours of housekeeping. Gustav, left alone in a totally new environment, bid his companions farewell as they boarded the *New York* to set a straight course for Diomede. Laura would be waiting for them with fresh home-baked bread if they found the island and could get ashore. Gustav, however, didn't feel sorry for himself—as comes through so clearly in his letter home to Norway.

"Nuokan, Siberia, 25 September 1923.

"My Dear Family,

"Peace through the blood of Jesus! As it is written, 'He is our peace who has broken down the middle wall of partition.' When a person partakes of it, he experiences the truth of such phrases as "peace like a river," and "peace that passes all understanding."

"My heart rejoices to be placed in a situation where I can realize the above to its fullest. How beautiful to belong to Jesus! Completely safe, free from worry, even though by myself among a primitive people of whom hardly one has grasped what Christianity is all about.

"Two factors stand out to me as almost overwhelming. First, the unreasonable fear that seems to pervade every facet of living; second, the barrenness of the land itself. Mountain tops white with snow tower above me. Below slides another sharp mountainside, maybe three hundred feet lower than the town, where an ice-cold sea beats mercilessly against a helpless coastline.

"In the house where I'm sitting, a kerosene stove gets us by for minimal cooking. With a mind of its own, it gives scant warmth to the room, preferring to send its heat up through the tin roof. I've been forbidden to work for four days, can't even pick up a pencil and write (which I'm doing anyway). Maybe I can at least read.... Nevertheless, my heart is filled with joy and praise for, as the song says, 'Where Jesus is, 'tis heaven there.'

"Am I sick? No, fresh as a fish and eager to get to work. It's just that yesterday the men brought a big whale to land. The poor folk are so bound by superstition that work must cease for all 310 inhabitants of the village, and I mustn't do anything either.

"At first my mind wrestled with their restrictions. Now I feel that the Lord would have me take it easy and use this opportunity to talk with the people. When I said something about how ridiculous these taboos are, several agreed and expressed hope that an upcoming generation might slip free of this bondage. I explained how back in my fatherland we take whales without such formalities and no bad luck follows. Perhaps some eyes are being opened. But now it's so cold that I must crawl in bed....

"September 27: Restrictions lift tomorrow so we can work again. Going back to when Høijer left me here in Nuokan, I haven't felt like a stranger. To the contrary, it's as if I am with my own people. Besides, I've been too busy to indulge in self-pity. As quickly as the village folk could bring tons of goods up the steep bank and into the house, I hurriedly stored them away. Then it began to snow. By six o'clock it was getting dark, therefore urgent that I choose my men. I asked one who understands English to act as interpreter. I meant to hire three or four workers until we completed the foundation of our new building. The headman thought I needed more because of winter moving in on us.

"'Maybe six?' I ventured.

"No, much too few. He suggested ten. I asked for those interested in working to step forward and immediately I had my number. The next day eleven showed for mustering in.

"Oskodeak, the headman's foster son became my special servant. He stays with me—cook, housekeeper, and man

Friday. Oskodeak and I relate like old friends though we don't understand a dozen words of each other's language. One cannot expect the best meals cooked by a young lad, but he learns quickly. Whale meat he fries better than I can, water he can boil. He makes pancakes and washes dishes. What more do I need?

"Our first work day began before eight o'clock with mud and slush at its worst. Hacking away with the simplest of axes and spades, they went hard at it for about three hours. By then everyone was soaking wet and wanted to quit. That I had nothing against! When skies began to clear in the afternoon, several of us picked up our tools again, completing sod work against one wall before it began to freeze. I tried to cancel work for the next day, Sunday, but when it turned out to be a fine day, a small crew came anyway. I explained as best I could what Sunday meant to me....

"Then the headman came to my room. In fragmentary English he approached me with wise counsel amounting to this: 'Winter is at the door, and we must get the house ready. When the ground freezes, it's hard to work with the few tools we have. It's right for you to keep Sunday and to rest. We Eskimos on East Cape have no Sunday, but some day we will have. For now it's all right for us to work when we see it needful, so let us go ahead even though you wish to be quiet.'

"With that piece of down-to-earth wisdom I gave the men my go ahead. For their first taste of Christianity to be equated with Sunday as primarily a sorry break from work that needed doing wasn't in their best interest. We must keep our priorities straight. The Bible clearly states that the Sabbath was designed for man's sake, and not man for Sabbath's sake.

"While the others began digging for a small outbuilding, I walked out on the tundra. Before long a boy came after me, and I soon realized that I had to be there to give direction. Actually quite a bit got done that 'day of rest.'

"Monday the wind picked up and only a few workers came. I was thankful as big crews do less than they promise. Though my interpreter was away, those able to put some English words together in logical order informed me that a whale would be brought to land soon. Another enforced holiday. I made plans accordingly, thinking that if I stayed more or less out of sight nobody in all that hullabaloo would miss me. I'd redeem time with my own carpentry.

"Along toward afternoon the wind carried a shout from over the sea. Immediately my handful of helpers deserted me, but curiosity led me out to a point where I could see a skin boat coming toward the beach. The whaling captain seated in the bow lifted high his harpoon with a big chunk of blubber—the signal for the crew to stop rowing and join in a rousing yell. Their shouts, which sounded like "hurrah," continued until the boat scraped land and the captain jumped out. The boat backed away, lying motionless for a long time. Apparently they were waiting until the man in charge came with fresh water, reindeer meat, and other things for an offering.

"For the most part I understood little of what was going on. Least of all, I understood myself. I only wanted to throw myself down and sob without knowing why.

"When the boat at last drew into shore to stay, the crew took everything out, carefully laying a piece from the whale's mouth to one side. After another long wait, the captain began ceremoniously stripping the reindeer meat. He laid a small piece in the whale's mouth, placed another in the back of the boat, and the third he threw out over the sea. Finally he laid a portion in an old fox head fastened to a stick above the gunwale. I learned later that the skull had been handed down from father to son for many generations, supposedly assuring the family line successful hunting. Their hunting god.

"Next the captain poured water over those pieces of reindeer meat, using the cup he brought from the house. Then he drank from the cup before handing it to an older man (maybe a shaman?) to drink. The rest he spilled out. The women brought reindeer meat, flour, sugar, and greens to eat while the men dealt out meat and blubber to everyone. At the water's edge another ritual was going on for a lad who for the first time had set his harpoon in a whale. I saw more than enough to leave me feeling heavyhearted.

"I scrambled up the bank and to the village. My servant had brought a fine piece of whale meat and was already preparing our evening meal. I turned to my toolbox with intentions of picking up where I had left off. I should have known....

"Here came the headman. In a most serious manner he let me have it: not a sound of saw, ax, or hammer should be heard from for about four days. The whaling captain would advise me when they lifted the ban.

"Gradually I was able to analyze some of my earlier impressions as the pressure of heathen atmosphere drove me to desperate prayer. I also wanted the Lord to show me what my attitude should be, what position I should take—I who put no faith in either fox skulls or idleness. Again I sensed that I must respect the office of the headman by obeying his order. The Lord can make evil work for good.

"Thus it came about that the bored and restless congregated in my room or followed me around. It was a great time killer: watch the stranger and listen to his stories. The interpreter, Ajuajuk, filled his role like a pro. With glad heart I took advantage of the long hours to sit and tell them about Jesus.

"At times they became so taken up with what I had to say that they laughed aloud exclaiming, 'The first time we've ever heard the like!'

"Ajuajuk went with me to ask the whaling captain when I could begin working—partly because I wanted a heart-to-heart talk with him. I tried to explain that trusting in an old fox head for luck and believing in spirits to give them whales was only a trick of the devil, who wanted to rob him of real success and happiness. The one true God whom I worship owned all the creatures on land and in the sea. When a person turns to Him with his whole heart, he can ask for what he needs, even whales.

"The man, obviously keenly interested, challenged, 'But if I don't get a whale, I'll think you are lying.'

"'Well, you just try Him,' I countered.

"'I think you're a good man,' extending his hand to grip mine with a hearty handshake. Friday I could get back to work. We parted with warm and mutual respect.

"Whale days became blessed days with no reason to bemoan lost time. I met with another positive aspect of the occasion climaxed by a feast outdoors. With nothing else for fuel, the natives burned whale blubber under the cooking pots. We all filled our stomachs with delicious meat and muktuk (the fibrous layer between the skin and underlying fat of the whale) until we were more than satisfied. Afterward, the headman and I went into several homes to greet folk and see how things were going. At one place we were asked to stay for tea—my privilege to sit on the floor as one of the family and savor what they offered me. Though hardly using any salt themselves, they set it out when they learned my preference.

"I recall the first time the headman invited me to eat in his home. It was all I could do to get the food down while praying for help to overlook the fingers and eating habits I wasn't used to. Unappetizing and absolutely non-Norwegian. Now I genuinely enjoy relaxing on the skin floor polished by much wear and dipping into the trough with the others. What's so bad about that?

"The headman also likes to come to my room for western food. 'Me too,' and without further invitation he sits down and helps himself. Once he and his wife came when I had just begun eating mush with only a serving for myself. No matter. Taking the dish between them, they cleaned it up while I did without. Tarajuanga and I are friends who can give and take; he's looking forward to visiting me on Diomede next summer. I must cook a big pot of mush for him and his companions. He says it's easy as his worn down teeth can hardly chew tough meat anymore.

"Sunday, September 30: I'm in Tarajuanga's house, older people grouped around me. It's difficult to hold heat in my thin board house with only a kerosene stove. I brought a candle to supplement the dim light of the oil lamp so I can write. Tarajuanga invited me to sleep here, but I'll go back when I get warmed through. With my own bedding plus the reindeer skin and sail he gave me to use my first evening in Nuokan, I can keep warm through the night.

"It's remarkable how that old man does all he can to show me favor. He's there to hold a board while I saw, or stands around just in case I need him. Though not expressing a spiritual hunger, he nevertheless appears to enjoy my company. Since the first time I ate with him and asked the blessing, someone in the family always asks me to do so before we eat. Once when we were seated around the food trough and conversation turned to the Lord, the headman ventured, 'Maybe *Angajon* [God] likes Eskimos too?'

"I assured him that God does!

"The people enjoy my attempts at learning new words and triumph over each one I master. 'You soon be good Eskimo,' they say.

"I like to hear their small votes of confidence because I do want to be one of them. I recall that over six years ago the Lord gave me Psalm 2:8, 'Ask of me, and I shall give thee the heathen for thine inheritance, and the uttermost parts of the earth for thy possession.' This is like the opening of a door.

"Now let me describe our mealtimes: Vaaminga, the headman's daughter with only one arm (her left arm was shot off when she was a child), comes to tell her father and two brothers that *kajok* [the meal] is ready. We enter the tent through the entryway where the dogs are lying. I get down on my knees so someone can brush off the soles of my heavy shoes as they wish to save me the task of unlacing them whenever they slip off their more easily removed footwear. Inasmuch as the skin hanging directly before us isn't fastened to the floor, we lift the closest corner and scoot in. At first it seems dark with only three oil lamps in a nine by fifteen room with a six-foot ceiling, but gradually my eyes become accustomed to the twilight.

"I crawl across the room to my assigned place against the far wall, Tarajuanga to the right of the lamp, I to the left. Tarajuala, his oldest son's youngest daughter, wants to be my special friend. She's a sweet child, about a year old, completely naked and with a big stomach that seems to overweigh her at times. Little wonder she works so hard at taking her first steps.

"Vaaminga sits at one end of this improvised table, dexterously carving meat and fish with one hand. She scoops up a nice heap, spreading it along the trough within reach of all. Afterward she sets out spoons and bowls of thick soup made with broth and flour, then a dessert of tea and sugar. No jaded tastes here, but that will no doubt come when their economy allows imports.

"Vaaminga also bakes a kind of bread over a small kerosene primus, so once in a while we have a crust of dry bread with our tea. She sits and sews skin boots with needle and sinew, giving the impression that she works with three hands rather than with one hand and two feet.

"October 7: Because of heavy snows the past several days, I haven't looked for the *New York*. Other than the roof, most of the carpentry is done. We have no roofing material, so the snow has fun sifting through the cracks and filling much of the room. My large work force wasn't happy about the layoff during those first whale days, but I saw already that we didn't have sufficient material to complete the job. Besides, it cost the mission far too much. There will be many brisk days for whoever winters here!

"Visitors sit by the hour watching me work. Almost everything I own has been carefully examined, not least my magnetic razor. Once I put some saw filings on a piece of paper to show the men how a magnet moves them. They were fascinated and later examined the cutting edge ever so carefully. I wonder if they thought it bewitched. I don't share just to show off what we have—I share because I thoroughly enjoy the people.

"These fine young men I see as brothers in Christ. Some want to learn to write. With our limited paper supply, we've resorted to using the packaging of Swedish hardtack I'll eat later. Occasionally I play the mission's folding organ, and to my listeners it makes little difference whether I sing in English or in Norwegian. Nevertheless, to show their appreciation they may come with a special portion of meat.

"Jungaten, the headman's oldest son (or foster son) is a dear fellow, true as gold. Quiet and dependable, almost shy, he is always looking out for my welfare. I never worry about my tools. Jungaten takes care of them. My wet clothes and shoes may disappear for a while, then appear warm and dry. One day Jungaten opened a box of bacon from the mission supply, and though I didn't know what he was up to, I let him go ahead. From the box he made a table as he realized that sometimes I got tired of eating with my plate on the floor. I accepted his work as sort of a thank you for something. Later I learned that it was his finger I had bandaged a couple months ago on Diomede.

"October 12: The *New York* at last! Several messengers hurry in with the glad news, but sea waves beating high against the shore forced the boat to seek another spot for shelter. Steep cliffs prevent their coming to us on foot, and it may be days before the sea calms enough to make connections. Though not the easiest assignment, I count it an honor to have been able to build on the first mission house in east Siberia. I'll count it as grace too when I get back to my dear one who waits on Diomede! We really don't want to be apart the whole winter, though I've tried to tell myself that it might have to be so....

"October 14: I'm on the rolling sea again, having left East Cape in a hurry last evening. The *New York* finally came, but its coming was also a letdown. To begin with, the crew endured nightmares since we last saw them. A strong wind blew them to the Alaska mainland where they were marooned nine days before getting out again. As the storm continued, Høijer encountered even more problems. Not least, the best interpreter for the job has a family that refused to accompany him to Siberia—so of course he wouldn't come either. Finally, Høijer himself decided he would return to Sweden and visit his family whom he hasn't seen in years.

"For all my efforts, we have no one ready to move into the house. Much of our wares we put back on the boat. The rest we left behind, hoping the outlook will be brighter next summer. I can't describe the disappointment written on the faces of the people. With sad heart I said good-bye to the natives of Nuokan—leaving them to face winter's darkness and the even deeper spiritual darkness that broods over the land. Dear folk, when will their day come?

"October 15: Last night we wound around in blackness trying to find the Diomedes. With no lighthouse, buoy, or birds to guide us, we gave up our search and drifted until daylight. Then we spotted our island in the distance. Hold the eagerness! Wind and waves won't let us anchor, so we had to go to the lee side of Big Diomede. Do we wait out the weather, or will the young Eskimo interpreter Høijer brought and I be put ashore here while the boat pushes on toward Nome? If the latter, we might have to stay until ice forms a bridge over to Little Diomede. And how long might that be?—at best a bleak outlook.

"I'm thankful that in spite of rough seas, I'm holding up fairly well. But I'm too weak to read the bundle of letters Høijer brought me, other than one from my brother.

"Now it's settled—my interpreter and I will go ashore to stay until we find a way home. So I'll close this long letter and send it with the mission schooner mail. I know you will send friendly thoughts over the sea and prayers of faith to God for us who look forward to winter life on an ice desert.

"Greetings to relatives and friends so far as you reach.

"Yours Kept by His Grace, Gustav."

12

Big Diomede

━━◆━━

When Gustav and his young interpreter went ashore, the local headman offered them lodging. It appeared that they would have instant rapport as the headman, in his early forties, already stood strong among his own people. He spoke English well, having traveled with a whaler down to San Francisco. Though they had much in common and often chatted, Gustav never penetrated an undefined aloofness. They remained friends and, at the same time, strangers.

Discomfort added to Gustav's loneliness. After five days of sleeping on a hard floor plus eating food that didn't exactly agree with him, all he wanted was out of there. Watching local residents coming home after a summer on the mainland needled him. If they managed to make it across that strip of water, why couldn't he and his helper find a way? He felt cheated.

"I had no right to blame them personally for being unwilling to row us over to our island," he confessed in a journal entry. "Still, I squirmed...."

With others crowding into the headman's house, the pair found lodging in a larger dwelling with a tunnel entrance. They smiled when given sleeping benches three feet above the main floor. Coming up in the world! Being allowed to cook their own meals, Gustav bought food from folk who had just come from Nome. Unfortunately, winter rations included an abundance of denatured alcohol bought (supposedly) for their primus stoves. When the alcohol intended for the stoves was mixed with liquor, vicious drinking sprees followed. Then, to these outsiders' dismay, another storm picked up in intensity, lessening chances of a quick trip home.

Though he caught cold and his upset stomach got worse, Gustav still tried to assemble the villagers to give them God's Word. Having never been in a meeting before, most of them had no concept of how to act in a somewhat structured group situation. But when the two outsiders began to view something as being not exactly proper, they had to correct themselves. What if they had grown up in cramped quarters with no privacy whatever—and with guests who didn't seem to know it was time to go home!

Interest spans, too, appeared unbelievably short. The story of Jesus dying on the cross was barely finished before someone started a card game. Gustav had seen this before, an obsession with cards equal to a craving for liquor—almost as if the two went together. One of the worst was a medicine man who some weeks earlier on Little Diomede had asked the Nyseters to read to him. Afterwards he knelt and repeated the Lord's prayer. Now he behaved no better than any other angry drunk did.

City or village, each has its own atmosphere—personality quirks perhaps, and sometimes of a spiritual nature. The political scene, even to local leadership, may also contribute to these differences. Gustav sensed that Big Diomede lacked a certain element of discipline that held the Nuokan people together. Exactly what, he couldn't pinpoint. Summarizing his weeks on the larger island, he wrote, "When the powers of darkness raged, I could only humbly bow myself and accept the experience as a lesson. It gave me a glimpse of what it meant for our Savior to come to fallen man who saw no need of Him. Though our days on that island weren't the most pleasant, they drove me to a place of entering into the fellowship of Christ's sufferings. I also learned that by centering my thoughts on Him, much of the oppression lifted and my downcast soul revived.

"I thank God for placing me where I have had to come face to face with desperate needs. The Macedonian call, 'Come over and help us,' is often seen or felt rather than heard. An inaudible cry for help."

Friday, October 26th, dawned a beautiful day. Gustav hurriedly searched out the headman, offering a better-than-average price for someone to row him and his assistant over to their own island. Inasmuch as this might be the last such trip of the season, plans were already underway with two boats going. Without waiting to see if there was room for them, Gustav motioned to his helper, "Come on!" and they piled in.

With the village being on the west side of the larger island, seven or eight miles of water lay between them and home. Everyone started out in top humor, but about half way over the wind picking up put them in danger of having to turn back. Someone suggested that Nyseter ask God for fair weather.

"Believe me, I never waited for their suggestion," Gustav whispered to his interpreter, who rolled his eyes and grinned.

In spite of heavy swells, the boats made it safely over. Gustav leaped up the bank and rapped at the schoolhouse door. He received a slow, "Come."

Entering the room, he found Laura alone. Having re-signed herself to her husband being away for the winter, she stood and stared as if seeing a ghost. Yes, she saw the two boats coming, but recognized only Big Diomeders. Her mind had blocked out anything more.

Once the couple started talking, they couldn't stop. So much news to catch up on! An Eskimo teacher had come. Having no family with him, he would use the main room, the Nyseters the two rooms above. While busy shoving furniture and reorganizing, Gustav tried to plan the spiritual side of their work, how best to adapt to their new role with an interpreter.

Among others, he visited an older woman with tuberculosis. "Poor Katinga," he said to Laura, "tired of living, but afraid to die. Natural reactions maybe, but she can't seem to grasp what I say about our hope of heaven. Her house is one miserable heap and the care she receives—"

"You call that care?" Laura shuddered involuntarily. "There she sits day after day, curled up in a ball with only the light and warmth of one seal oil lamp. What she coughs up gets smeared around where it falls."

"Katinga appears to be listening when I talk about the love of Jesus," he continued, "but as soon as I'm through, she begins talking about what means most to her. Bring a little of this and a little of that. Not least, she's begging again for alcohol to help light her primus."

The primus, a small kerosene burner about nine inches in diameter and barely a foot high, required alcohol only to get a fire started. Gustav puzzled. How could people spill and waste alcohol like that? Still, one must help where he can. He brought Katinga more alcohol, painstakingly showing her and her family how only a few drops gets the primus going. After many drops, facts began to add up. Mixed with liquor...how naive could he be? After that he had to say no to her pitiful pleas for "alcohol for the primus."

Like any other community, Diomede produced honest, straightforward citizens, a credit to their race. Nonetheless, the Nyseters ferreted out part of the hospitality shown them as being "fine hay to make the cow give milk." One man blurted out his disappointment with, "We don't like poor people."

The Nyseters understood, but what could they do? If only their neighbors would accept the spiritual riches they offered. Perhaps eyes long accustomed to darkness find it hard, even painful, to open to the light.

Gustav and Laura Nyseter.

Schoolhouse on Little Diomede, 1920s.

Diomeders

Harry Soxie, Ruth, and the Nyseters.

East Cape Eskimos in front of Tarajuanga's house.

13

Winter: 1923–1924

---◆---

Aware that in time he and Laura would absorb the
lifestyle of Diomede, becoming one with the community, Gustav continued his word sketches while
details still grabbed his attention.

"Thinking about our surroundings (both positive and
negative) brings praises to my lips even before I write. We
have so much to thank God for! Basically this is a peaceful
place, even though the real peace of God may be a foreign
concept to most of the local residents.

"On the plus side: we're never annoyed by rude visitors,
no rats or mice to disturb our food supplies, nor a cat to steal
anything. No moths to make holes in our woolens, no mos-
quitoes, no uncomfortable heat to plague us in summer.
What's necessary to hold body and soul together has been
provided along with the Lord's mercies, new every morning.
LOTS of fresh air both outdoors and indoors, for it seeps in
easily through these thin board walls. Water we can get right
outside our door. Granted that it might taste a bit salty, but it
has come in solid form a long way over the sea before getting

frozen against our shore. Our fuel supply isn't exactly un-limited, but still more than we thought we'd have.

"An uncommon bonus came about mid-November when a north wind blustered in a mass of driftwood just ahead of the pack ice. The natives took what they wanted. We also worked energetically for several days retrieving wood that the waves kept snatching from us. We played a fair game, but the sea with a 'Take that!' soused us with spray. Sticks and logs doubled their size with ice, most of which we knock off before carrying them indoors. The rest of this glossy coating melts away as our daily ration lies beside the stove. Combining dry wood and coal with this generous contribution sent by the Lord gives fuel enough to hold us until summer if we're reasonably sparing.

"One day we took the thermometer, which registered minus thirty-four Fahrenheit outdoors, into our sleeping room. Minus two indoors! Luckily, we have warm bedding and keep our heads well protected lest we waken with a mean headache.

"Minimal snowfall and fewer storms make it possible for the hunters to get plenty of seal. It's a pleasure to watch them coming home, dragging their prey by a rope fastened in its muzzle. The smooth, shorthaired seal skin glides along like a sled. In fact, they can hook their dogs to their catch and ride high! Hunters get everything from birds to polar bears, but are least likely to bring in a walrus. However, when pack ice moves north, we may see a herd of those majestic crea-tures lying on the ice floes. Though not easy to get close enough for a handy shot, clever hunters have been known to bring home a prize providing food for the entire village.

"We get some of their bounty by trading 'store bought' stuff for their meat—preferably fowl. Of seafood, their crab is the finest. The reindeer meat we had expected to get from the mainland stood on the 'Sorry, I forgot' list along with other supplies (at a dear price!) ordered via the mission boat."

Gustav commented on their house fellows, the teacher, and the interpreter. As a staunch member of his own denomination, each held his ground. Having encountered that same brand of loyalty back in the old country, the Nyseters looked on and smiled, confident that the teacher would never let it become a serious issue. Gustav spoke of him as being one of the finest men he had ever met. Having taught on the island before, old and young alike knew and respected him.

The interpreter, barely twenty years old, had lost both parents and sometimes acted like a spoiled child. Though obviously insecure and lacking roots, he created no problem among the people. Possibly, Gustav reflected, the isolation coupled with the strain of interpreting, his mind continually switching tracks, demanded more than he could handle at this time in his life.

To save on fuel, the missionary team often went to the largest house in the village for midweek services, entering via an underground tunnel leading to a hole in the floor of the main room. The two such dwellings on each of the islands served as gathering places for storytelling and card playing during the winter. Their first meeting began in spite of several games in progress. Soon, however, the card enthusiasts moved elsewhere. Better yet, Aiahak, head of that home and the most avid player of the bunch, became a believer. From then on he stayed for the meetings.

After New Year's, one of the medicine men came with questions about salvation. He was unhappy, ready to give up his old arts, he said, and would no longer ask people to come to him for their ills. Though the Nyseters thought he meant well, they nevertheless felt cautious lest it be food politics. Then he slipped—concluding his "confession" by asking if he could get mission supplies on credit. On basic principles they had to say no. Only Hoijer decided matters that concerned mission funds. With that, their would-be convert turned away to carry on business as usual.

Though common usage makes the title of medicine man an acceptable term, it is really a misnomer. Somewhat a professional, the shaman's or witchdoctor's "cures" usually involve curses or adjuring evil spirits. Supposedly accomplished through a ritual stimulated by the steady beat of his magical drum, he gives a prophetic message addressed to those present. Sickness, he claims, can be scared away by wild screams—as much as his throat can stand. An honorarium, reckoned according to the patient's possessions, must be paid in advance. The practitioner might get a dog or a gun for his efforts, a steep demand in an economy based on subsistence living.

A few headmen, especially in Siberia, exercised a constructive influence. In contrast, the shaman ruled by fear, constantly trying to present further proof of his skills or his contact with the nether world. Gustav was told that one of them had plunged a long knife through his heart, so far that the point came through his back. He had pulled the knife out without leaving a scratch. Shaman influence, however, reminded Gustav of a tired moon, its power waning—a fact which became more apparent when outsiders viewed their demonstrations.

One of those leeches especially drew Gustav's pity, for he saw in him traces of a once-handsome man. But, as the story goes, his brother bit off his nose in a drinking orgy. Sin laid other ugly stamps on him too, leaving him nearly poverty stricken, his home life soured. When Gustav tried to tell the poor fellow that the devil is a hard taskmaster, he never replied to the contrary. Neither did he express a willingness to change. One question haunted the Nyseters: What might his life have been if someone had reached him for the Lord in his youth?

They couldn't change the past, but they could reach out to an upcoming generation—like the boys who came in the afternoons for Bible club. Independent of an interpreter with this group, Gustav counted those hours in lively discussions his special joy. They also had regular meetings which hunter Aiahak continued to attend faithfully. A few women came, but what they really grasped seemed less certain. Confined much of the time to one room, seldom meeting anyone from the bigger world, their mental capabilities had been less challenged.

Weeks grouped into months. Checking the almanac in the middle of April, Gustav let out a loud *"Huttetu!"* (an all-purpose exclamation equal to "Boy, oh boy!").

"What?"

"Spring, Laura! Spring! What kind of irony is it to call this north wind frolic the herald of summer?"

Ah, but they did have one sure sign: daylight from early morning until seven in the evening. Their rooms being on the north side of the building, a thick layer of ice covered the window, so on a relatively mild day Gustav decided to let light in there too—even if by force. With considerable effort he got the inner window off, then scraped until he made a peephole. The next morning a half inch of new frost decked his hard-earned opening.

Having to dry their wood before they could burn it contributed to the frost problem. But, as a splinter of diversion, the wood of a certain deciduous tree added more than moisture. When "toasted" it sent out a nostalgic aroma that reminded one of the pleasure of going to the barn, though there wasn't a farm animal on the entire island. The smell, neither pleasant nor unpleasant, triggered more than one, "Remember when...?".

Cold weather hung on longer than usual. Why? The natives had their own suspicions. Did they forget that last Thursday they heard, instead of the sounds of school going on, the sounds of saw and hammer? The teacher had been making a coffin for poor old Katinga, who had died the previous evening. No surprise—all were amazed she had held on that long. During her last days she couldn't seem to keep warm, so her brother gave her a wool blanket. Wrapping her body in the blanket, relatives had laid it in the chest along with a lamp and other small items. Later they would visit the grave with more things to help her along her journey into the next world.

The family had called for Gustav to officiate at a funeral held in her eight-foot-square house. After his brief talk, they nailed the coffin shut. Because the doorway was too small, they fastened a rope to the chest and got it out through a window in the roof. Then began the long haul up over cliffs and boulders—pulling, pushing, lifting, shoving until they reached the designated location. For lack of loose soil of reasonable depth, they placed the casket between stones and left. Thus ended Katinga's earthly story.

Within twenty-four hours, a fierce storm moved in with a steady drop in temperature. Some of the people expressed concern that the corpse wrapped in a blanket might be too warm, thus bringing on bad weather. Fortunately, no one suggested doing anything about it.

The teacher later recalled a similar incident. An old man, tired of living, pleaded to be hanged. Someone called the head teacher who tried to talk him out of such an idea, but no. He had one desire however—a real burial when he died as he didn't like the idea of hungry dogs carrying his bones around the village. Inasmuch as casket material wasn't available before the Department of Education provided such, he would be proud to be the first to be laid in a box. At three in the morning someone knocked at the schoolhouse door—the old man was gone. The teacher nailed together a coffin, lined it with thin cloth and called for help to lay the man in it fully clothed. Immediately after his burial a blustering storm lashed out against the island. Instant logic pointed a finger at the lined box, which in turn generated talk of opening it to remove part of the lining. When the storm ended, the talk also stopped.

Winters were hard, often cruel, and this one had been no exception. But spring did come, as it always did, preceded by its vanguards, the migratory birds. In the distance, great herds of walrus lazed in the water. Hunters, however, could only look and wish as they were unable to buck the strong winds. The ice between the islands held firm, though Gustav declared he would just as soon blow that bridge in two if he could. Inasmuch as American law didn't apply on Big Diomede, some of those addicted to home-brew went to the bigger island to make it. Not that anyone enforced the law at home, but perhaps they felt less guilty celebrating on foreign soil.

A bitter north wind made the newcomers wonder if those first migratory birds had made a mistake—until the last day of May, when a tardy spring hustled in all out of breath. Winter did a hasty retreat. The air burst with clouds of small sea birds wending their way back to nests still decked with snow—the better housekeepers among them chattering angrily. Best of all, the pack ice moved out, breaking Big Diomede connections and opening the door to the western world. There's a certain sense of separation intrinsic of islands that to some people becomes almost unbearable. Through the long winter, however, these two Scandinavians had been cocooned in a miracle. Isolation may have been an inconvenience, but never a major problem.

"Laura, let's take a walk. I don't know how far we can go, but surely farther than we have been all winter," Gustav had suggested.

Together they ambled toward South Gate, as they had named the lower tip of the island, reveling in the sneaky thrill of getting away without anyone knowing. Not that it mattered—just the fun of doing it. And, not least, they could escape the narrow confines of a village to inhale a change of scenery.

Their eyes shifted focus. "Look!"

Who said it first? Too plain to be mistaken for anything else, a mast sticking up over the ice ridge moved in closer. While Eskimos were mooring the boat, the captain stepped forward to greet the Nyseters in excellent English, introducing himself as the teacher's brother. He had come to take him back to the mainland and had also brought a sack of mail, much of which was for Gustav and Laura. Forget the birds!

"How can we describe getting mail after seven or eight months of playing Robinson Crusoe?" Gustav asked. "Some of our letters were a year old, but nonetheless—or all the more—dear to us."

14

Summer Again

W ith the opening of boat traffic, scores of mainland Siberia Eskimos paddled across the strait in their umiaks to visit and barter—Gustav's opportunity to repay the hospitality he had enjoyed during his stay in Nuokan the previous year.

"I confess mixed feelings," he stated candidly. "I get tired of constant begging and bargaining, while at the same time I'm overwhelmed with the privilege of presenting the good news of salvation. Not to be minimized is the renewing of acquaintances—people who will always live on in my heart."

Early in June the Nyseters spotted a three-master and a four-master pushing through the ice, both after large sea animals. The ships loaded with all kinds of wares to trade were headed for the northernmost points of Alaska and, weather permitting, Canada. They lay offshore for a day before lifting anchor. Shortly afterward, one of the villagers handed the Nyseters a large paper bag with, "It's from Pedersen on the *Nanuk*."

The couple stood there like two living question marks with big eyes. No mistake, it was for them. Peering down at beautiful apples and oranges, they speculated: Did these really come from California? Or perhaps straight from heaven?

Later, upon hearing that the *Nanuk* (Eskimo for polar bear) lay at the edge of the ice again, Gustav hurried over South Gate to personally thank the captain, one of his countrymen. After thirty years in America, English and a smattering of Eskimo had replaced his mother tongue. Pedersen's versatile background included several winters with Roald Amundsen and other explorers. His wife, a nurse who had worked at a mission farther up the coast, accompanied him on this trip. While her husband traded with the local folk, she updated Gustav on the outside world and its current events.

At a convenient break, the missionary asked about buying a few supplies. Pedersen promptly ordered a young man to get what Gustav wanted and more, including fresh reindeer meat, potatoes, and fruit. Gustav tried to hide his nervousness—what if he didn't have the cash to cover it? Nonetheless, he gladly accepted the Pedersens' invitation to stay for dinner, knowing that Laura would understand.

"When the day was over," he told her later, "and I asked the price, the answer was a warm smile and one word, 'Nothing.' Here I stood with almost more than I could carry, and his wife handing me a sizable roll of newspapers. Those people!" he said as he shook his head. "God's people, I'm sure," Laura added softly.

Though the couple had felt neither lonely nor deprived on Little Diomede, it was as if this stimulating contact roused them from a winter's hibernation. With a twinge of nostalgia they watched the *Nanuk* as it swam westward between icebergs for continued trading. The island itself, however, wasn't totally ice-free until July—a big plus for the men who crawled over ice to the ragged cliffs where they gathered eggs. The birds build their nests on the most difficult ledges to reach, but Gustav quickly learned how to hold his life with one hand and gather eggs with the other. The men took mostly bantam-size eggs belonging to a type of sea gull. Put down in oil, these would keep a whole year.

Egg gathering with its dangers and corresponding camaraderie tapered off the hunting season; animals must have time for raising their young. Restlessness gripped the village—to Nome they would go. Boats pulled out, leaving Gustav and three other men with a number of women and children. As for occupation, the missionary stood outnumbered with two of the fellows being shamans. The third, a widower, was reported to have shot his wife some years ago, but the Nyseters weren't anxious. They felt only good will.

Clear days usually brought visitors from the Siberian coast. A Coast Guard cutter and an occasional trade ship nosed against their island; the school boat that looked after the teachers and their supplies also stopped a couple of times. Though enjoying those brief contacts with the world they used to know, the Nyseters still scanned the horizon. Where was the *New York?*

Høijer had indicated he would be returning before fall....

Early one August morning, the familiar putt-putt of a diesel engine awakened a sleeping village. How delightful to see their old friend who had spent the winter in Sweden! But, no, he couldn't stay. He must go on to Nuokan to check on mission supplies.

A couple days later the veteran returned with a vague report. Obviously he didn't feel like talking. His young boatman, Paul Sarv, chose to offer details. Upon overhearing that the *New York* was to be confiscated, they had slipped away under cover of darkness. The men had poled and rowed between ice floes until well out of sight and sound.

When they finally deemed it safe to start the motor, the boat itself acted as if bent on making trouble. That along with the ever-uncertain elements was enough to break a strong man, but not Høijer.

Not Høijer? Perhaps, because he had always seemed so indestructible, they said it out of habit. Unconsciously they may have put on, or increased, a burden of keeping that image. Now the older man's silence made them wonder if his visit to Sweden had lacked too. What about his son who seldom saw his father during his formative years? Were there hidden hurts? Possibly, with home fires reduced to embers, Høijer felt compelled to fan the one desire he had left—to rekindle a flame in his beloved Russia. Those who knew him best looked on with genuine concern, admitting that, yes, they did see him cast down at times....

As a pleasant interlude, the mission received a distinguished guest, the Danish-Greenlandic explorer Knud Rasmussen, who knew the north like none other. Besides speaking both Danish and his mother tongue fluently, he had the rare gift of a bilingual thought pattern. Dogteaming from Greenland across the ice to Canada, he continued traveling along the north coast, taking time to adjust to dialects along the way. Having completed years of intense research in arctic Greenland and North America, recording both history and legends, he crossed over to Siberia. There the Soviets cut his work short, expelling him because his permit had been delayed en route to those remote corners. He stopped at Little Diomede on his way back, a deeply hurt and disappointed man. His invaluable studies of northern native cultures were never to be completed.

The missionaries readily agreed with the explorer and his view of life across the strait as expressed in his book, *Across Arctic America.* "Until the American Bureau of Education commenced work in Alaska, the Siberian Eskimos were greatly superior to the American, both in conditions of life and in general estimation; now, however, the reverse is the case and those Siberian natives who have been in Nome for trading purposes marvel at the enormous progress made by their fellows on that side, while they themselves live in a country whose government seems to take no interest in them whatever beyond getting their furs at the lowest possible price" (p. 378).

If one of our media happened in on Knudsen's brief stopover on Diomede, he might have quipped, "Ah, summit of the Big Three." A Swede who loved Russia with a passion; a Norwegian who had been there only weeks, but felt its heartbeat; and a Danish-Greenlander who was kin to the natives of Siberia from where, centuries earlier, his mother's forebears had come. Each felt an indescribable bond, an affinity with other peoples of the north, and understood what cold, hunger, and long nights can do to even the strongest among them.

So went the short summer on Diomede. While its people were returning from the mainland, flocks of birds began winging their way south. Visitors likewise spoke their farewells. Gustav and Laura, however, were buoyed by the prospect of Højer's Eskimo interpreter, Harry Soxie, staying with them. Nowhere could they find a better worker than this middle-aged man whom they described as "well built and of worthy manners." His father had been a headman who, because of some serious charges against him, had to flee for his life. Whether guilty or not, sordid rumors worked hardship and a deep insecurity on his family who lived in constant fear of revenge.

When Harry got out on his own, he had associated with white people who dragged him still farther down. He joined a church as "the thing to do," all the while going deeper into sin until concerned missionaries dealt with him personally.

The young man recognized his need and surrendered to Christ. He served in several capacities in mission work on both sides of the strait, and the previous winter attended a Bible school in the states. His wife, daughter of a headman, their fourteen-year-old son, Franklin, and fifteen-year-old daughter, Marie (a deaf-mute), accompanied him. Though it meant a lot of give and take, the teacher generously allowed both families to use the kitchen.

In a letter home, Gustav referred to their own improvised tent in a storeroom, heating stones to warm their bed before they crawled in, as "an arrangement that cramps our style a bit."

Then he added lightheartedly, "A lot of togetherness, but we can make it!"

15

Second Winter

—◆—

Gustav's journal entry introducing their second winter began with an indefinite comment about how, being human, our reactions to any given situation may vary. What "given situation" did he mean? Perhaps the constant inevitable adjustments that accompany living under crowded conditions.

However, the occasional tension between house fellows that marked the previous winter had vanished. By rights the schoolhouse belonged to the teacher who continued to use only what space he absolutely needed for himself. The Soxies had the larger area in the main room so they could function as a family. The Nyseters got the corner farthest from the stove, nearest the outer door which, Gustav declared, had made a secret pact with the north wind. Most of the locals weren't in the habit of shutting doors as the usual curtain at the end of the tunnel closed itself. The Nyseters, envisioning splinters of brittle glass from the small windowpane skidding across the floor, got up repeatedly and shut the door. To insist that the children do likewise amounted to "Slam it!" That they couldn't afford.

Though sturdy, the building lacked insulation. Washing and drying clothes in one room created enough moisture to glaze windows, walls, and floor with ice. The real rub, however, had to do with Harry's wife being a skilled skin sewer. Fine, except that she tanned hides herself. As part of the process, she laid skins in old urine, leaving them until the lye content licked off the hair before hanging them up to dry. "Going all natural" sounds great, but nature reaches its limits too. Gustav complained that his nose literally burned, but where could he go when the wind whistled to the tune of forty below?

With that he composed a riddle: "We have a light (as opposed to dark) house, for the walls are glossy white. Light also comes through the opening to the south. What is it?"

Answer: the icehouse. Blocks of ice stacked for their winter water supply served as a windbreak as well as providing them with a temporary outdoor utility shed. Let the winds howl, for there he hardly heard it through meter-thick walls. He enjoyed the solitude, whether in calm reflection, sawing wood, or doing other chores in the one place he shared with no one else. His until the ice was gone.

More than once Gustav cried out, "Lord, you must give us a place to ourselves if you want us to stay longer on this island."

God's call or no, he seriously considered leaving. But how could he? For the first time they were beginning to get the basics for Bible study across to the adults. Also, he and Laura had finally begun learning the Eskimo language. On the negative side, some of the Diomeders ridiculed Harry's teaching because he spoke a different dialect. "That's not our language," they taunted.

The Nyseters, who still stumbled over English and struggled fiercely over Eskimo, entertained doubts. If the people rejected Harry, what about them? In a better moment, however, Gustav set his journal straight. "No, neither we nor Harry hear complaints all the time, for we do have a precious faithful few—cream of the crop. We have seen some changes too in the face of death. One woman who reached out for the message of hope made a clean break from her old ways, holding true until the day she died.

"Because she had openly confessed Christ, I suggested a Christian burial. Her son-in-law halfway agreed, then behind my back arranged for a heathen one. I didn't make an issue of it. After all, the ceremony could in no way affect her after she was gone.

"I'm finding out that, though denied or otherwise hidden, people do engage in a form of idol worship. The East Cape folk in their simplicity allowed me to see their offerings last fall, but here they take 'little things' when going hunting. As I see it, a polar bear head hanging high on a whale bone in the village is a kind of god too. Right under it, we've heard, is a lucky place to be sitting if a man wants to shoot an animal swimming by. It borders on droll humor to see a man put water in the mouth of a dead seal and say, 'Come again,' lest he offend its spirit. His courtesy serves as a safeguard, appeasing a spirit that supposedly enters another animal he might want to take later. Hunters whisper among themselves lest an animal spirit hears and gives away their plans. If a man gets a hole in the sole of his boot when ready to go hunting, it spells bad luck for the entire crew. Sprinkling seal oil on graves ensures favorable weather. On and on it goes.

"Just as a horseshoe over a doorway in Norway fails to bring good luck, so will a token like a glass bead or a reindeer hair sewed into the seam of a garment fail the one who trusts in it. I've pondered: Where do we draw the line between idolatry and superstition, or is there a line? I haven't arrived at solid conclusions. I only know that the human heart is difficult to fathom and in this our dear islanders are no different than the rest of us."

Of more serious consequence, the people embraced a hazy concept of life after death. One's final destiny depended largely on the manner in which he died. The worse his death, the better his chances in the next life. Perhaps that belief lay at the root of their penchant for reciting horrible endings.

The Nyseters were told that shortly before they arrived, a young man in his skin boat was being tossed around by the breakers until onlookers despaired of rescuing him. No one seemed shocked when he grabbed his hunting knife and stabbed himself in the heart, which they considered a far more noble death than that of a simple drowning.

A neighbor also related that in his youth he had to kill his sick father, who didn't want to be a burden to his family. Desiring a grand entrance to the eternal hunting grounds, he chose to be stabbed to death. Inasmuch as a close relative must carry out the deed, this son had been chosen— and he could not refuse. The father sat up, naked to the waist, and with his left hand pointed to his chest.

"Stick here," he ordered. And in went the knife.

"No, you never got it right." He pointed again. "Stick here," he said, and once more the bloody steel went in. The man's hand dropped down. He was dead.

Inasmuch as others related the same story, it might be accepted as fact. If not, their rehearsal of the gruesome account could be interpreted as a way of coping, accepting severity as their lot—existing under the most adverse conditions, constantly fighting the elements and without hope....

The father in another home became very ill, presumably with tuberculosis. At the family's request Gustav and Laura visited the sick Elasanga. Encouraged by his wife and mother-in-law, he expressed a desire to know the Lord. Not recovering immediately, he resorted to witchcraft—giving his gun as advance payment. His family, until then one of the cleanest in the community, cooperated by subjecting themselves to a long list of rules such as don't bathe, don't comb your hair, and don't work.

Of course these didn't help. Finally Elasanga asked to be carried over to the other island, possibly because a shaman works better without opposition. That same day the mother-in-law called for the Nyseters to come. There at the house they found the wife also sick. Though baptized Catholic, both women admitted they hadn't lived for God and wanted to turn their lives over to Him. After an old-fashioned salvation meeting, the wife threw the clincher, "Now we can have a bath!"

Some time later, the husband came home, wiser for his experience. He too gave his heart to the Lord and, like his wife, got well. From then on they stood out as one of the most responsible families in the community.

Not least in the power of the gospel is how the Nyseters and the Soxies could live so confined without strained relations. They followed their own interests and, at the close of each day, met for devotions. Often Avvak, also known as Charlie, stayed to share this time with them.

One morning this fourteen-year-old son of Aiahak announced that the previous evening, March 7th, a new little member had joined their family. A few days later word came that the parents, who couldn't afford another mouth to feed, were considering giving away the infant, Jamani.

The Nyseters wanted to adopt the girl, so Gustav went to present their offer. After some discussion between father and mother, a long silence followed. Then Aiahak with one word, *E-ee* [Yes], and a nod settled the matter.

The parents agreed to the Nyseters taking the baby home March 19th. With no shopping on Diomede, and certainly no baby showers, Laura made a layette from their own worn cotton garments. When the day arrived, Gustav crawled through the tunnel, stuck his head up through the hole in the floor of the earth dwelling and asked, "Where's my girl?"

"*Damna* [There]," the mother said, pointing to a bundle of furs in the corner. At Gustav's request, the thirteen-day-old baby tasted of her mother's milk once more. Then he gently tucked her under his warm coat and crawled back out of the dusky room.

With tender emotions he handed the child to his wife who sat ready with the baby's bath water. "Here comes a birthday present for you!" he beamed.

After bathing and dressing her in clean soft garments, they held a little dedication service, asking the Lord for His gentle, loving care over their special treasure. They named her Ruth after the girl who left her own people to become a beloved daughter in the land of Judea.

Though the baby seemed to thrive on canned milk, she cried most of her waking hours—and she was awake a lot. Her new parents couldn't find any reason for it, though she seemed more content when taken out for fresh air. One day Laura put Ruth on her back under her parka, Eskimo style, and walked around the village. Neighbors were horrified. Didn't they know they were inviting evil spirits to take note of the child. Why didn't they keep her hidden?

When it became apparent that Ruth suffered no ill from the many outings that followed, this bit of superstition gradually changed. Only a few die-hards labeled her as different, reasoning that evil spirits backed off because of her being in the hands of white people.

As Ruth in baby fashion made her needs known, the Soxies gladly squeezed closer together to help make room for her. Even the clothesline went through changes with diapers and blankets demanding priority. School children had to run in and see the youngest before classes began—while she herself gurgled and kicked in response to all the attention. Within weeks, their crybaby proved herself as lovable a child as anyone could ever want, a constant source of happiness.

16

A New Home

After holding out as long as it could, winter's pack ice receded into the vast uncharted regions between the Bering Strait and the North Pole; the air quivered with the cries of millions of birds laying claim to their summer homes. The sun, though staying behind clouds for a while, shone both day and night as if trying to buy back the winter months. Local residents kept pace, living the short summer to its fullest.

Nor were the missionaries a whit behind. With umiaks from Siberia coming and going almost around the clock, they seized every opportunity to call people together for meetings. When the bell sounded, listeners packed the classroom, overflow sitting on the floor. Listening to Laura's beautiful voice carrying the gospel right into their hearts, they expressed a delighted, "Mrs. Nyseter big sing!"

Gustav noted, however, something different in the demeanor of their visitors. Smiles came less readily. Strange troubles were brewing across the water. They hated their overseers. They complained about poor management and a shortage of food. They weren't allowed ammunition enough for hunting; rumors compounded that it was being spared for use on them, the natives.

A Russian steamer was supposed to be on its way to East Cape right then, and if things got worse, they declared, they would revolt and get rid of as many of their oppressors as they could. After that, they themselves could be killed. Half resigned to such a fate, they justified their intent, "Best to end it all right away. Something like that happened a hundred years ago and we know it can happen again."

They probably referred to the conquest of Siberia in the eighteenth century. When taxes to be paid in furs weren't forthcoming, the authorities wiped out an entire tribe. Enraged natives tried to retaliate, but uprisings were quickly and forcibly squelched.

One Bible story Gustav told made a marked impression on the bitter, frustrated people. They listened open-mouthed as he recounted how Israel had called on God when crushed beneath the iron fist of Pharaoh. Oh? Then maybe this God could do something for them too, for all Siberia's downtrodden folk. Gustav moaned his helplessness. Unable to see beyond their immediate distress, they missed the main point. Did they only want God as their rescuer so they could live as they pleased? The missionary nevertheless continued to encourage them to reach out first for the peace that comes with sins forgiven, to find their heart's rest in Jesus. Thereby other blessings can flow.

By mid-August the stream of summer visitors had tapered off and the Soxie family moved on to a new assignment. Sacks of coal lay outside the schoolhouse and Gustav wasn't sure what to do with them. The Department of Education had written a friendly but pointed letter: Vacate the building they had used for two years as the teacher would be bringing his family with him.

That left the Nyseters in want of a house while the elements tried their faith. But exercising faith sounded like a poor answer when mischievous fingers of the sea reached out to play with their coal supply lying close to the beach. First it rolled some of the canvas sacks almost up to the schoolhouse. OK, that solid stuff could stand a tossing. In fact, Gustav thought it fascinating to watch the water handling those heavy sacks like a pro. It ought to go on exhibition!

Then it went too far. Like a deliberate, underhanded plot in motion, the sea sneakily picked at the gravel below the pile, carrying their priceless coal away from their door. Enough is enough! Gustav dashed out and began working like a wild man. A passerby seeing his struggle came to his aid in a very dangerous work. If overtaken by a wave, they could be sucked out to sea and lost. When they fought for footing to keep the wind from blowing them over, ocean spray evened the score by soaking them to the skin. At last, with the loss of only two sacks, they counted the rescue a success. Yet Gustav still didn't know what to do with the coal. Should they give it to needy families, then find their own way back to the mainland?

"We've received an ultimatum," he reminded his wife. "We can live neither outdoors nor in an icehouse this winter. Wouldn't even the best builder in the world scratch his head before trying to put up a house here after fall storms have begun?"

Laura smiled. Her husband was the best. "Then scratch your head. We have that used building material Høijer left here a year ago. You know he'll never take it to Siberia."

"Look, dear, I know more about carpentry than you do. It's utterly impossible for anyone to build with what we have on hand. I say it's impossible!"

Impossible. But when Gustav approached the village fathers for permission, they readily gave him an abandoned site on which to build. Common sense told him to respect his neighbors' years of experience, building partly underground for the benefit of earth insulation. Alas, his Norwegian blood stirred again. This time it tricked him into thinking he must have some kind of cellar for storage. In the middle of his project, however, clouds moved in with more than average rain. Water poured into his half-dug cellar, while he idly watched it run out as fast as it came in. So much for that old-country idea.

Gustav paid dearly for the hours lost. His pitiful lumber supply got soaking wet and, for lack of proper tools, his work took twice as long as it should have.

"Laura...," he began.

"How about a cup of coffee? Here, you hold little Ruth while I slice the bread. In a few weeks our family of three will be moved into a home of our own. I'm so thankful to God—and proud of you."

How can a man hold out against that? Laura, always able to see a brighter side, buoyed his courage. It was the sixth of September and four walls up when they saw a boat coming, one they didn't know. As it came closer, they recognized a man on deck—the unpredictable Høijer with a larger mission boat, the *Ariel!* The last the Nyseters had seen of him, he had just fled Siberia. From Diomede he had gone south to Seattle to recoup both strength and courage for one last effort to get into the land closest to his heart.

How Høijer cheered when he saw that the Nyseters hadn't thrown up their hands and quit! Gustav accepted his congratulations while wrestling with mixed feelings. His enthusiasm didn't quite match Høijer's, for it looked as if he had begun his work both too soon and too late.

Why didn't that guy come weeks ago? Because of new material he brought, Gustav had to redesign the house, doing some of his painful carpentry over again. Of course it wasn't all bad. The uncanny old Swede, somehow anticipating their needs, also brought doors, a stove, and slabs for the chimney—items that couldn't be bought or scrounged on either of the islands.

When Gustav got back to his carpentry, it went better than he had dared hope. Besides the much-needed material, Høijer brought a young man, Victor Carlsen, to help. After a few hours on the job, Gustav enthusiastically reported to Laura, "Lazy is he not!" Victor's youth and eagerness swept in like a fresh breeze from heaven. Not least, though American-born, he also spoke Norwegian. Hallelujah!

The last of September the mission folk moved into their half-finished house. At the same time an advantageous wind forced the school boat, the *Boxer*, with representatives from the Department of Education to seek shelter near Big Diomede for several days. Thus these men, one of whom had written the letter requesting that the Nyseters vacate, failed to arrive on schedule. The delay enabled the Nyseters to get completely moved before these visitors came.

The *Boxer*, a legend in its own time, deserved a lot of credit, servicing village schools, transporting teachers and supplies. A cruise could run as much as eleven thousand miles as its captains habitually took on more than ordinary line of duty. Typical of what that crew and boat did on the side was a trip to Wainwright, where the people were out of fresh meat. The *Boxer* took five skin boats and a couple dozen Eskimo hunters about twenty-five miles off the coast to look for walrus. Not only did they get what they went after, but when they anchored off a huge ice floe to take on fresh water, the natives killed the largest polar bear ever recorded in Alaska (nineteen hundred pounds).

When the boat, this time delayed by weather, arrived at Little Diomede, the Nyseters met the gentleman who asked them to move out of the schoolhouse. They had the distinct pleasure of inviting him to dinner in their modest dwelling. They found him to be one with a heart open to the natives' welfare, one who would become a friend and helper to them too.

Gradually, Gustav, Laura, and Victor were able to complete the finishing touches inside, making the little house cozy and comfortable. A real home at last. With this one more goal reached, they unwaveringly affirmed, "The Lord does all things well!"

17

Co-workers

—◆—

Høijer's Seattle sojourn had actually initiated the first lap toward his final attempt to reach the Siberian coast. Besides working with the Swedish Mission Covenant, he was also known as founder of the Slavic Mission Society of Stockholm and moved freely among various church groups. He had home-based in a Lutheran mission in Seattle while looking for a vessel to replace the aging *New York*.

One day Victor Carlsen walked into the room where Høijer was lying down, resting. Victor's heart went out in compassion to this man who, like the apostle Paul, bore marks of suffering for the cause of Christ. On impulse Victor asked the older gentleman if he could do anything for him.

"Yes. I'd like to have a bottle of milk."

Victor hurried out to the store, and returned with milk for the missionary who held it in his hands and thanked God for His provision. That short prayer of thanksgiving reached through to the wayward young man who, though brought up in a Christian home and active in a church youth group, had viewed its teachings as someone's uneducated guess. Determined to find truth on his own, the inquisitive youth dabbled around with books on liberalism that appealed to his intellect. The ensuing confusion met its deserved end when he finally talked out his bewilderment to the older man, who gently led him back to the Bible.

When Høijer's strength returned, he combed the harbor where lay the *Ariel*, a fifty-foot motor vessel that had once been part of the equipment of the battleship *Pennsylvania*. After getting it towed to the August Brauer place at Poulsbo, his boatman, Paul Sarv, and others helped strip it down, rebuild it seaworthy, and install an eighteen-horsepower engine. On a beautiful summer day in 1925, friends gathered for the dedication of the new mission boat, wishing its owner and the crew of six plus one passenger Godspeed.

For Høijer it looked like a dream come true. Stopping only long enough to pick up last-minute supplies, he headed north through Canadian waters and on to Ketchikan. There Paul Sarv, who had been with him on his previous trip to Siberia, left the ship, returning to Poulsbo to take Mildred Brauer as his bride.

At Høijer's suggestion, the adventurous Victor had decided to go along to winter with the Nyseters; the fellowship of mature believers would be a boost to his faith. He sat by the hour, weather permitting, reading his Bible and other Christian books on board. Arriving at the island, Victor felt as if he had come home at last. He later described his stay in the far north as heaven on earth. "There I learned the real meaning of Calvary, that Christ died for my sins. I burned my books on liberalism (we used them for fuel to fry our hotcakes) and asked for Bible studies with Gustav, who was a tremendous teacher. That year changed my life."

Without doubt, the young man filled a gap for the Nyseters. The Eskimos were at home with their own culture and language; the Swedish Covenant workers on the mainland composed a colony in themselves. The Nyseters, however, communicated in their mother tongue only with each other or an occasional trader. Perhaps a sense of this hidden hunger had prompted Høijer to bring unsolicited help to (as far as he knew) an already overcrowded schoolhouse.

In Gustav's words, "When we heard Victor speak Norwegian, we about flew away to Mount Delight! Besides our immediate family of three and now Victor, we also welcomed Ruth's older brother, Charlie, who had expressed desire for Bible training. The mission paid for the fellows' board, but we ate together as one happy family.

"Our house, twelve by fifteen feet, became quite crowded with us and an accumulating store of earthly goods. Compared with our neighbors, however, we had space to spare. Later we enlarged with several fine rooms—pantry, wood shed, gymnasium, and carpenter shop built of ice blocks or packed snow. Never mind what we'd rather have. We liked and appreciated what we had, making the most of these outdoor additions until the latter part of March when mild weather weakened their walls."

The young men weren't in the house so much as to be under foot. Victor often visited the big island to teach both children and adults. The Nyseters' little home, a touch of paradise, offered space in which to relax or study during the day and to hold classes for new believers in the evening. Charlie proved to be a promising lad, while little Ruth stole hearts—blossoming into the whole island's darling. The Nyseters counted their blessings by the handful.

The two sacks of coal lost in the storm got more than repaid by a stinking whale that drifted ashore before pack ice moved in. Gustav smiled at himself—he who had looked askance at the Siberians using blubber for fuel. The frozen chunks burned exceptionally well and with no smell when sandwiched between wood and coal or placed directly on the fire.

An excerpt from one of Victor's letters describes the gift of the whale. "The coal and the whale. There's more to it than that. One of the big miracles I experienced in my life was God's amazing supply. The coal unloaded off the *Ariel*, less than five ton in briquette form, pulverized in the damp climate. Though it gave little heat, we had to stretch its use for Sunday services as well as our own daily needs. Driftwood was scarce and winter was coming on.

"Then a cry from the villagers—we thought a late trading ship had arrived. Instead, a large black whale had drifted ashore, presumably wounded by whalers and escaped to die. A roundup of able-bodied men with knives and axes advanced on the carcass. Soon women well accustomed to manual labor carried loads of thick blubber, probably six to eight inches thick, to the village ice cellars.

"After taking all they wanted, they told us at the mission house to help ourselves. Gustav and I stacked up blubber, more than a cord of solid fat, on the beach. You should see how that stuff sputtered, sizzled, and burned in our little stove! It only took a brick of it to cook a meal and warm the room. Every day we thanked God for such a timely and perfect supply of winter fuel."

The material aspect of village life seemed to parallel the spiritual tide, both moving steadily upward. Even the elements threw fewer than usual tantrums. Spring followed with great flocks of cranes by the thousands passing by on their way to colonies far to the west. Of other winged creatures, millions. In the ocean, whales and walrus were almost milling about. The polar bears made their escape north, except for five that the Eskimos shot—partly in revenge for having wrought havoc with several skin boats out on the ice.

The other side of the Bering Strait opened exceptionally early, allowing the first influx from Siberia to reach the
island on May 20th. Leaving their boats at Big Diomede,
they crossed over on the ice bridge. With them came a Russian teacher, only twenty-two years old, who had spent the
winter in the house Gustav had worked on. Though a far
cry from what Hoijer had in mind, it nonetheless served
Nuokan's youth. At least they could learn to read. During
his forty-eight-hour sojourn to the free world, the teacher
stayed with the Nyseters. In spite of their best efforts, however, communication was practically nil.

Conversation with the natives fared better, for they had
learned each other's expressions, understanding more than
words said. Gustav was thrilled to learn that the man he
had challenged to drop witchcraft and believe God for a
whale did just that—and came in the winner!

Shortly after this contingent left, three fugitives from
Russia arrived. One, a doctor obviously not used to physical labor, stumbled in totally exhausted from exposure after grueling days of camping out, his elbows bent from
rowing through icy waters in an open boat. His muscles
were so taut that his fists were almost closed. Victor had
to feed him until he built strength enough to hold a fork
and drink from a cup. Whether from a bad conscience or
fear of a firing squad no one knew, but he turned pale as
death at the sound of a boat nearing the shore. The doctor
later made his way to mainland Alaska without having
disclosed the secrets of his past.

The Nyseters themselves became so used to traffic that
boats coming and going no longer caught their attention.
Then one afternoon two girls, a teenager and one consid-
erably younger, walked in. Were they really from Siberia?
Gustav and Laura looked at them, then at each other. The

older girl appeared to be of mixed race, the younger showed stronger Chuckchee traits. The one with the more European features startled them by stammering out a few Norwegian words, explaining that they both had been in Norway. Her name was Camilla Carpendale and the other was Anita Amundsen, foster daughter of Norway's hero, Roald Amundsen. They both expressed childlike devotion to the explorer who had shown them kindness and hoped to see him when they got to Alaska's mainland. But how did the girls get to Little Diomede? The story goes back a ways....

Amundsen, a key figure in arctic exploration, had sailed the *Gjoa* along the north coast of North America, proving the existence of the Northwest Passage in 1905. Later, wanting to verify some of his theories about ocean currents, he planned another expedition for which he had the *Maud* built in Norway. Avoiding the danger of World War I mines afloat in the Atlantic, he sailed up the Norwegian coast and through the Northwest Passage to the Pacific. The journey took two years, during which time he was forced to winter off the Siberian coast.

From a nearby Chuckchee settlement, Amundsen chose five men to accompany him on an upcoming expedition. One of them, Kakot, asked for leave of absence to travel several days' journey north, explaining that after he lost his wife, a cousin took his little daughter. Having heard that this tribe was suffering for lack of food, Kakot feared his child was starving—which Amundsen could well believe. Foodstuff from his stock on hand was keeping the local tribe alive that winter.

Kakot received permission to go, but failed to return at the end of his allotted week. Three days later, however, the tired man stood on the ship's deck at dusk. "What about the child?" Amundsen asked.

The father pointed to a bundle of furs near the railing. At Amundsen's command the man picked up the bundle and gave it to his captain, who carefully unwrapped a five-year-old girl, naked and every bone showing from starvation. Her body was covered with sores, her hair alive with cooties. The explorer ordered proper care, and within weeks she looked like a different child.

When the ship stopped at East Cape, they met an Australian trader named Carpendale, married to a Chuckchee woman. Inasmuch as the couple had several children, Amundsen asked if their nine-year-old Camilla could travel with him and little Takonita, whom he called Anita, to Norway for schooling. The girls became like sisters and when Camilla returned to East Cape two years later, Anita went with her.

As the Communists gained control on the east coast, the storekeeper Carpendale read his fate. He and his wife must make one desperate effort to escape. They clothed their children, Anita included, with all they could wear plus a few hidden treasures hung around their necks. In the dead of night the family slipped out to their boat carefully hidden around the bend. Rowing silently lest they be heard and fired upon, they moved between ice floes and headed eastward.

When they reached Little Diomede the following day, Carpendale's gratitude knew no bounds. He stumbled out of the boat and onto shore where he knelt and kissed the rocks. Safe at last! The children of course, not realizing the dangers they escaped, scrambled quickly up the bank to announce their arrival.

It went well for them as later in the summer Captain Petersen of the Nanuk took the family to Nome. Because of Carpendale's Australian citizenship, they moved to Canada. With the help of missions connections, Camilla and her sister, Molly, went to Poulsbo, Washington, to live with the

Brauer family. Mildred Brauer Sarv (wife of Hoijer's former boatman) who was caring for her parents while her husband worked in Nome, gave the girls her room.

Years later Mildred reminisced, "It was interesting. We had the two girls, but always felt there should be one more. When asked if we would take Anita Amundsen too, we were most happy. Somehow we just knew there should be three, and now the number was complete. Those were good years with the girls in our house, going to school, adding life to the old home place."

Victor, returning to the Northwest and keeping in touch with the Brauer family, reflected, "I know this for sure, that the slow-speaking, overly quiet Anita was transformed by those secure years staying with Mildred and learning—as well as by her own personal encounter with the Lord Jesus Christ."

After the Carpendale family moved on to begin a new life, the Eskimo teacher who had served his people so well for three years, accepted another assignment—he and his fine family leaving a real gap. Who would take their place? The Nyseters could only wait and see.

Later in the summer, an outstanding archaeologist, Diamond Jennes, specializing in Eskimo life and culture, visited Diomede. During his weeks there, the company of this pleasant man offered another refreshing break from everyday routine. Just before he completed his studies, two Danish botanists sent out by the Canadian government arrived. Incredible as it may seem, they were able to identify at least eighty-three different kinds of plant life on that barren island!

The most difficult farewell came last. Their friend and co-worker, Victor, also went his way—taking warm memories with him and leaving just as many behind to encourage the Nyseters through the dark months ahead.

18

A Sad Aftermath

⟡

Summer on Diomede had been the greatest, but what about Old Høijer? The *Ariel,* his dream come true, seemed destined for trouble almost from the start of their voyage out of Seattle. Upon reaching the estuary of the Kuskokwim River, its engine failed. Otto Antonsen, a Christian sailor who had quit his job on an offshore light ship to go along as engineer, managed with a few meager tools to get it going again. Were it not for this extra crewmember recruited at the Lutheran mission, they would have shipwrecked on nearby reefs.

After leaving Victor at Little Diomede, they headed for Alaska's mainland. On the way, a near hurricane battered the ship, breaking one of its masts. Unable to count on help from the sails, they dropped anchor to wait out the storm.

Putting together fragments of the story, Gustav concluded that some of the men on board hadn't been able to handle the suspense....

They insisted on going ahead, and Høijer, with a reputation for being in command no matter what, appeared to be losing his grip. Surely he knew all too well the danger of shallow water along the desolate, unmarked coast of the Bering Strait!

Apparently, however, the over-eager got their way. Without waiting for the gale to subside, they lifted anchor and set their course for Nome. On September 25th, in the blackness of a wild, stormy night, they ran aground where merciless waves tore into the helpless craft. The eight aboard made it safely to land but, as Nyseter commented, "*Huttetu*, what a night they went through!"

The incoming tide tossed up pieces of wreckage on the shore. With wavering torchlights made from rags soaked in gas, the stranded travelers found driftwood. Huddled close to a bonfire, they managed to absorb enough warmth to keep from freezing to death. Daybreak brought little relief, but did verify their position: east of Cape Spencer, far from any town or village.

The group stayed together on the beach. As strength allowed, they sorted through flotsam, seaweed, and spume to salvage what they could of personal possessions. Then Ernest Bohman, a university student from Troy, Idaho, who had taken a year off from his studies to experience an Alaska winter, offered to go for help. Following the coastline he could make the estimated hundred miles to Nome if all went well. It wouldn't be easy, but with Høijer's careful directions he had reason to start out with confidence.

A few days later a passing vessel spotted the shipwreck and offered assistance. Though Høijer obviously needed immediate medical attention, he held his position of command, refusing to leave the site. Karl Von Lensburg, their one passenger, agreed to go ahead to officially report the tragedy. In his place, the ship left two native men to continue salvaging what the others, too weak to care any longer, had abandoned. Upon receiving news of the *Ariel's* fate, the Coast Guard immediately dispatched a launch to pick up the survivors along with the two ship's helpers.

In the meantime engineer Antonsen, a younger man, stepped forward to take responsibility for looking after the sixty-nine-year-old Høijer. Upon arriving in Nome, the veteran of many a stormy voyage was suffering from exposure and exhaustion and had to be hospitalized while waiting for the next passenger ship south. Later he and Von Lensburg whom the missionary won to Christ while on the beach, journeyed together on the *Victoria* to Seattle for further medical attention.

At the time of their departure, twenty-three-year-old Bohman still hadn't reached Nome. In response to a telegram from his father, a rescue team set out to look for him. The two older men might never have been told that searchers found the young man's body near the mouth of the Tissue River. He had given his life in a heroic effort to ford the stream on his way to get help for the others. On November 25th, two months after the shipwreck, Høijer also went home to his reward, his body laid to rest in Washelli Evergreen Cemetery in Seattle. Von Lensburg followed him only a few days later.

Gustav responded to news of the tragedy reflectively. In all honesty he admitted that one can't help but wonder why their important mission connection to far shores should be cut off so tragically. Høijer had such great plans for reaching new areas for his Master. "The real answer," Nyseter summarized, "lies beyond our understanding until we get to the other side, where everything stands unveiled in the light of eternal values. For now, ours to say, 'The Lord's will be done.'"

In a way Gustav's words could be labeled as a typical response from Norwegian fishers and farmers of that era.

For the most part, they were either fatalists or staunch men of faith—the result of harsh elements turned loose, leaving them with palms upward, holding nothing.

When pressed for further comment on the fate of the *Ariel* as relating to mission endeavor, he replied, "It doesn't affect any of our decisions. We're Pentecostals who work closely with the Swedish Covenant Mission and will continue to do so. We have already made a practice of getting our supplies by whatever means that come our way as we can't hold a mission boat, or any other vessel for that matter, to a schedule. We will miss our friend, but we'll go on laboring for the Lord the same as before.

"Høijer's passing isn't reason to quit. To the contrary, his contribution to the sacrifice of life itself, gives all the more reason to press on."

19

Winter's Worst

T he summer of 1926, warmer than usual, gave vegetation a boost. Several men, Gustav among them, climbed approximately twelve hundred feet over the top and returned several hours later with their bounty. Gustav, after stumbling along with about forty pounds of harvesting on his back, his legs protesting all the way, made it home with a special touch of pride. He set his gunnysack down in front of Laura. "*Multe ber!*" she exclaimed.

In her growing-up years Laura had often picked them for her mother back in the old country. These cloudberries represented the finishing touch on desserts for festive occasions in north Norway—and a rare treat for visitors from the south.

The Nyseters along with the rest who stayed home that summer expressed concern for the islanders who had failed to return from their annual trek to Nome. Autumn had moved in and the weather wasn't exactly smiling down on open boats. Would the stragglers somehow get back before freeze-up? Well into October the school boat *Boxer*, true to its reputation, came bringing them safely back to their island.

The new teacher also arrived. Though pleasant to meet, this retired doctor and his wife, both in their seventies, immediately made it clear that they claimed no faith in God. They were strong in their own way and, unfortunately, some of the weaker characters buckled under their influence. Gradually the more responsible adults also began to waver with the reviving of heathen dances and the looseness that inevitably followed.

Nature itself held to its seasonal pattern. The ice pack, still at safe distance, made room for a herd of walrus to move in close to Big Diomede. The best hunters set out in a large umiak, others paddling along behind in their kayaks. Without warning, winds suddenly tore loose and forced them to seek refuge on the neighboring island.

The ensuing tempest, which Gustav described as making any he had ever known pale by comparison, raged day after day. The water boiled, seethed, and frothed until the whole fused into one vast stretch of white. At the storm's peak, the schoolhouse, built to withstand almost anything, shook under the impact. Much of the island lay crusted with ice formed of sea spray that froze as soon as it hit the ground.

With tremendous force the waves continued their relentless pounding, rolling huge boulders back and forth with an ugly, foreboding sound. Even the walrus seemed to fear its colossal might, their actions implying that the storm had carried itself too far. A big herd, staying in a spot just out from the missionaries' home where the billows weren't quite as fierce, often sank out of sight to escape the beating of the sea.

After a week of the barrage, the village awakened early one morning to an almost deafening silence. What was that eerie noise? Nothing but a deafening silence—everything so still that one felt compelled to speak in whispers. No more turning of the churn down on the beach. The pack ice that had pulled back in face of the storm had regained its position and with hushed command told the sea to cut the nonsense. Hunters returned empty handed, but without complaint. They counted themselves lucky to be alive.

Gustav had saved a newspaper article taken from a book, *God's Frozen Children*, by Harold McCracken, the caption of which read: "Lonely Island off Alaska Shores Must Be the World's Worst." A portion of the article read:

> There is probably no spot on all the earth where life unfolds in a stranger drama; where human isolation has been more complete throughout a larger part of its existence; or whose unknown history occupies a more significant place in the chronicles of our continent, than the two tiny rocky Diomede Islands in the center of the Bering Strait. It is there that Asia and America are but two miles apart; where primitive man had but two short journeys of twenty-five miles each in his skin canoes to make the first migration from the mainland of the Old World to the New, and where Eskimo culture is still retained....
>
> For untold centuries, within view of the Old World and the New, the Diomeders have led a hazardous existence on what are nothing more than two great piles of rocks. Throughout more than half of the year they are surrounded by the terrible turmoil of the mighty ice floes crushing and grinding their way through the narrow congested gateway of Bering Strait, which completely isolates them from all the rest of the world. Even during the periods when there is little or no ice around them, it is often impossible to land on or leave the islands for long periods on account of the terrific storms and "pea soup" fogs which add to the misery of the living. It is a place where the dogs eat the bodies of the dead and the offal of the living and where starvation stalks as a frequent visitor. And yet, in spite of all their struggles to survive, the Diomeders are one of the hardiest and proudest of all Arctic peoples....

"If his writing sounds colored," Gustav verified, "I'll add that it is not a bit exaggerated. In my own descriptions I have worked at using no color, trusting that facts speak for themselves. The cleverest mind and pen, however, can never accurately portray the barren, desolate, difficult conditions at earth's farthest ends."

Storms notwithstanding, for the Nyseters personally all had gone well thus far. Their family of three had hardly known poor health or sickness. One morning upon awakening, they heard the usual, "Good Morning," from Ruth's bed, which stood close to theirs. She wanted to crawl in with them, which they often let her do. When Laura lifted her up, she let out a sharp cry. They soon understood that she had pain in her stomach. For several days her parents carefully watched what she ate until she gradually improved enough to go outdoors again.

Ruth's favorite spot was the playground where she ran around with other children. After her setback, however, she didn't have enough energy to play. Laura took her there anyway to let her look on, then brought her home again to rest. She acted strangely quiet. Though not particularly hungry, she ate and afterwards managed to crawl up on a bench to dry a few dishes, "helping Mama." That she loved doing and wasn't ready to give it up. Not yet....

What followed is best told in Gustav's words. "That was the last time our Ruth would be able to move about. The next day she was one very sick child. We tried to believe for her healing, but while the rest of the world celebrated Christmas, we lay in deep intercession for our dear daughter's life. For forty-eight hours our baby battled pneumonia. Laura and I barely snatched winks of sleep in between caring for her and pleading that she be spared from the hand of death.

"Once in a while we heard her parched lips whisper, 'Jesus.' We knew Ruth meant, 'Let's pray to Jesus,' as it had always been our habit to pray with her before tucking her into bed.

"Now her only word was *Jesus*. When we knelt and prayed to the Children's Friend, our little wildcat (as her mother often called her) folded her hands and lay absolutely still until our 'Amen.'

"During her terrible sickness, whether conscious or otherwise, Ruth seemed instinctively to reach out for prayer. She seldom tried to talk, her dry, scratchy throat making it difficult for her to breathe. About 6:30 on the evening of December 26, we heard her utter the name of Jesus. Shortly thereafter the struggle for life was over. Our precious treasure, loved as much as ever a child could be loved, left us for a better land.

"I won't try to describe our feelings. It was as if everything was gone when Ruth was gone. The Lord had to take our child of promise because of our own folly. She, our treasure, had become like an idol to us who were more taken up with her than with Him. My wife and I had also nurtured a bit of pride in her being so healthy and full of life. It was our girl who found her way into the heart of everyone who saw her, be it one of the local citizens or a stranger to our shores. Our girl. How easy it is to accept honor that belongs only to God!

"We bury our faces in the dust with, 'So be it,' to Solomon's cry of despair that all our days are sorrow (Eccl. 2:23). Yet God's Word holds in spite of human frailties, and with Job we can say, 'The Lord gave, and the Lord hath taken away; blessed be the name of the Lord' (Job 1:21).

"With heavy heart I went out into the winter night to Ruth's first home. I crawled through the dark tunnel (that she never liked), stuck my head up through the floor, and said to her nearest of kin, 'Our little one is dead.'

"Though her family had tried to prepare themselves for the news, the mother let out a sharp cry. There had always been a tender understanding between her and the child she couldn't keep. I hurriedly backed down and out the tunnel, followed by the father who came to our home right way. He just sat and cried with us.

"The next day almost the entire village came to 'weep with those that weep.' We were surprised at how they sympathized with us and entered into our sorrow. Folk who heretofore appeared as hardened sinners sat torn with sobs. There was hardly anyone who didn't express deep, intense emotion. Their caring meant much to us.

"Some of the men offered to make a coffin for the little body, but we had already decided that we would use the white crib I had made for her. We didn't hurry with burial as is customary on Diomede. We waited a couple of days and held the funeral in the schoolhouse. After a song and a few words, everyone walked by to see that sweet face for the last time. A poignant interlude in our lives closed as strong arms bore our Ruth to her final earthly resting-place.

"In the middle of winter our sun can't rise to its zenith, but barely peeks over the southern horizon. It tried its best to cast a few pale rays over the Bering Strait while willing hands worked with stones, forming something like a little sepulcher around the earthly remains.

"When everything had been taken care of, I went around and pressed their hands in thanks. We don't sorrow as those who have no hope, nevertheless our humble home seems terribly empty after she who was our sunshine and laughter faded away.

"Only the Lord can fill the emptiness...."

20

Extended Family

W as it just their imagination, or was spring really slower coming this year? Hurts hung on. Gustav and Laura being equally wounded, one couldn't lift up the other when inclined to judge themselves too harshly. They desperately needed someone to embrace, encourage, and assure them that God wasn't punishing His faithful servants by taking their child. "For he doth not afflict willingly, nor grieve the children of men" (Lam. 3:33). But, overwhelmed by heartache, the couple seemed momentarily to lose that close awareness of His great compassion.

As if their personal loss weren't enough, all they had tried to teach the villagers for their spiritual and material welfare seemed to be going down the drain. Negative everyday happenings, ordinarily taken in stride, pushed the broken-hearted couple farther down. Soldiers of the Cross suffering from battle fatigue.

Summer began late. They watched their scant supply of staples dwindle to almost nothing after the annual Siberian "invasion." Busy adding a bedroom to their house, Gustav paid little attention to the first trader coming in July. So little to plan for now.... Early August, however, Laura reminded him that they still had a few weeks of summer left.

"Wouldn't you like to take a trip to the mainland for a breather?" she suggested.

"Couldn't we both go?"

"No," she replied with finality, remembering too many seasick hours. "I have no desire whatever to cross that unpredictable Bering Sea."

Laura stayed home while her husband took a trip to the outside world after four years of isolation. He sailed with a trader to Nome, then proceeded along the coast to visit places he knew from their journey to Diomede. Friendly folk everywhere showed genuine interest in the couple's well-being and extended their good wishes. After a month's vacation he returned home to find Laura at her best.

Gustav had so much to tell. "What a treat to see trees again! And the feeling of walking on flat ground! I almost didn't know where to set my feet. But next year, my dear wife, you will go with me."

Though Gustav and Laura had a happy marriage, the house seemed empty without Ruth and Victor seated at their table. Charlie too had left after only one winter. None understood what drove him, but when spring came he acted as if he needed to prove something. Perhaps he entertained dreams of becoming a big hunter. Whatever, he wanted complete freedom to go his own way. For all that, Charlie frequented the Nyseters' home and, during what Gustav referred to as one of his tame periods, expressed desire to be part of their family again. Of course they said "Yes." The chap showed much potential. Besides, he was Ruth's brother. The winter months went well, Charlie's abilities amazing them. He learned to read music, play the guitar, and use the typewriter, and he excelled in various other pursuits. But, when daylight hours lengthened, the restless one followed his usual pattern—this time gone for keeps.

That winter the Nyseters also took in an orphaned girl ten or eleven years old. Margaret had lived in a children's home in Nome, then somewhere farther south in Alaska before being placed with relatives on Diomede. She had gone through a lot. Scars from a gland operation marred her appearance; matter ran from one of her ears. The child's foster family had provided neither sufficient food nor clothing. She often stood alone against one of the buildings, ragged coat sleeves pulled down over her cold hands, watching other children play.

Laura pitied the girl. Shouldn't they ask her people if she could stay with them? When the other couple readily agreed, Laura rose to the challenge, making clothes out of nearly worn-out garments of hers. They only regretted that they had not taken her sooner.

One might have expected Margaret to be sad and withdrawn. To the contrary, she revealed a sparkling personality. Under the Nyseters' loving care she smiled almost continually, often bursting into a merry laugh. Though behind in most of her subjects at school, due in part to impaired hearing, she surpassed many of her classmates in other ways. When Margaret brought playmates home, the house resounded with laughter. Their presence reminded Laura that others needed special attention too, so every now and then she bathed several girls at once, washing their clothes as well. She and Gustav chuckled when they recalled the day they got carried away with the project and twelve dresses hung on their indoor line! Local folk placed little importance on laundry, especially in winter. Where would they put the clothesline with a half dozen people in a hut eight by eight feet square and a man's height at best?

Unfortunately, it added up to less then six months that Margaret thrived with the Nyseters, for when spring came she also wanted her own way. Her new guardians didn't mean to be too strict with her, but complete freedom amounted to lack of protection, perhaps even a question of morals. They simply couldn't allow her to stay out all night. As a result, the girl often played alone during the day while her companions slept. When they played, she slept.

Suddenly Margaret announced that she would rather stay with relatives in Nome. Of course the Nyseters couldn't deny her right to leave. However, she later wrote her regrets as her own people mistreated her terribly. Authorities again placed the girl in a children's home, where she died of tuberculosis. Thus another chapter failed to end the way they had hoped, but Gustav and Laura took comfort in knowing their second foster child left this world happy in Jesus.

Five years to the day since arriving on Little Diomede Gustav announced enough was enough. He had visited both Siberia and the Alaska mainland during that time; Laura had been no farther than to Big Diomede. She needed to get away. Surely a bona fide vacation of a few weeks couldn't be counted as too much of a splurge.

When the next whaling ship anchored off shore, Gustav contacted the captain. Would he be so kind as to take two passengers to Teller? The friendly man from Tromso, Norway, had no sooner agreed than they got their things on board.

"Laura," Gustav grinned, "I feel like school let out!"

"The price of our tickets?" they asked when under way.

"Nothing."

Within hours they walked the flat beach and homey by-paths of Teller where both natives and non-natives bent their efforts to make the Nyseters' stay pleasant. The town had its special sideshows as well. Roald Amundsen and his men had landed in Teller after their dirigible flight over the

North Pole in the *Norge*. Townsfolk kept an assortment of reminders from the world-famous expedition. One enthusiast went so far as to amass a huge heap of thin wire that had been part of the balloon's skeleton. But an exciting past wasn't all. Each summer the community revived a bit of the old glory with ships frequenting its port and an occasional plane flying in from Nome.

Reindeer grazed on the mountainside beyond the town. The Nyseters were invited to cross the fjord to see the annual reindeer count, at which time the owners hired cowboys to help tally them. This herd alone numbered over ten thousand—only a fraction, they were told, of those fine animals in the north. Besides local onlookers and tourists, four photographers flew in to film an event worth showing the big world out there!

Inasmuch as the Nyseters brought their own boat along with them, they spent hours on inlet waters fishing for salmon or whatever else would bite. Afterward they strolled leisurely along the sandy shore, picked berries, or went hunting for wild ducks and geese. Local residents complained about a cold wet summer, but for them it was unquestionably the best they had experienced since leaving Europe. (They also escaped Diomede's worst with both old and new snow in mid-July. Even the pack ice moved in early, hanging tight for several weeks.)

At Gustav's request, the Teller town council allowed use of their schoolhouse for Sunday meetings. Apparently the message of being saved by accepting Jesus as Savior and Lord came as a new concept for a fair percentage of the congregation, who listened attentively.

Back in 1894, Rev. Tollef Brevig of the Norwegian Lutheran Synod had gone to Teller to pastor a few families of Norwegian Laplanders who came to teach reindeer herding. In time, however, he became quite involved with the Eskimo village several miles away. Brevig and his wife, after months of nursing during the terrible measles epidemic at the turn of the century, started the Teller Orphanage to care for those left homeless by the death of close relatives. Later Rev. Brevig, with no one else to officiate, preached the funeral and performed the committal for his wife whom he laid to rest by their small son and daughter who had died earlier. The Nyseters listened to the Brevig story with pained appreciation. At least they still had eath other....

A gold-prospecting family, faithful attenders at the Nyseters' meetings, invited them to visit their home a few miles up the mountain. The buildings in their rugged setting reminded them of an old-country *seter* (summer cheese farm) among the green hills. Though these vacationers had spent a few years in "the land of gold," they had never seen the yellow stuff taken. With their own hands they lifted a spade of dirt and put it in a pan which they held under water, shook, and turned carefully until all the soil, sand, and grit washed away. Tiny particles of color lay on the bottom. Not many people, however, gathered enough of these grains to make it a worthwhile occupation. The rich pay dirt of Alaska belonged to an era fast slipping away.

After a delightful reprieve that stretched out to three months, the couple booked passage on the school boat to return to their island, ready to go home, but at the same time dragging their feet. Certain trends the previous winter had left them feeling disturbed in their spirits.

21

Lives at Stake

⎯⎯◆⎯⎯

T The *Boxer's* capable captain found a way through
dark and treacherous waters, bringing Gustav and
Laura back to Diomede on the tenth of October.
The pack ice, which had moved in and out many times
already, left enough of its inexhaustible supply to form a
miniature mooring basin just out from the village.

As the couple neared the island, the old excitement returned—home to pick up the work begun among a people
they had grown to love like kinfolk. In spite of disappoint-
ments, misunderstandings, and a few awkward encounters,
ties held strong. Definite changes had taken place over the
past five years. Young people who came for Bible club were
grasping spiritual concepts, seeing more to life than hunting and fishing. Without being coaxed, they knelt to pray
with their mentors.

Nevertheless the Nyseters struggled against a foreboding they couldn't shake. Then suddenly, like a festering sore
burst open, adults opposed the truth, callously bragging
about giving themselves over to the devil. A white Christ

show hunting favors? No way! They would rather turn back to witchcraft.

What sounded like rash threats began to take ugly shape. Setting out to prove that their hunting god would give them a whale come spring, they scheduled a "whale dance"—a whipped-up frenzy based on black magic. Because it had to be relearned from an old man on Big Diomede, a large umiak with several villagers rowed over there to receive instructions.

Upon their return, the adult population, stalwart Aiahak included, turned as one back to heathen rituals. In preparation for full rites, the two larger dwellings were turned into dance centers. In one of them lay Ruth's brother, Charlie. While far out on a hunting expedition, he had taken a bad cough that developed into tuberculosis. What if his last days were made more miserable or death hastened by cramming the hut with sweaty performers? Due to these close gatherings, the small pox epidemic also took an upswing.

"Sick children, babies fearful and crying, youth being caught in a net of sin. What kind of a god do they serve?" Gustav lamented. "Our God's graces come so rich and free, but the devil's wages are hard earned and cruel."

The man felt himself becoming angry as he watched people, desperate to please the whale god, subject themselves to six weeks of grueling rehearsals. Once they "passed their exams," the grind would culminate in a big feast when the village presented its appeasement offering. Violence, savagery, and mass hysteria took frightening control as the participants threw restraints to the wind. Shielded by the teacher, they expected no accounting for whatever took place.

The village chose to ignore the couple who stood alone— hurt at seeing heathen ideas, ancient and modern, joined in a vicious pact to destroy the inroads of the gospel. The sound of the orgy with its frenzied screams penetrated their walls.

"We've got to do something. We've got to stop it!" Gustav cried as he tried to cover his ears.

"There's nothing we can do, but pray," his wife sobbed, "and God knows we've been doing that for weeks."

"Maybe I should go over there, but how can an insignificant person like me put a damper on their revelry? Might as well try to stop the Niagara!"

The missionary had no desire to see such an exhibition of demon worship, and his going would no doubt be futile....

"I have to do it, Laura. I'm going. We haven't been invited, and I'm not going to announce my visit either. I'm just going. God help me!"

With long strides Gustav crossed the snow to the large house, crawled through the tunnel and up through the floor. He never told what he saw going on, but when the dancers' shrieks reached such a crescendo that it seemed to lift the roof off the building, he dropped to his knees. He could restrain no one, but he would withstand at least some of the demonic forces. Probably no one heard his voice above the din. Crying out alone at the top of his lungs, he begged God to show mercy toward those poor people. After a while he got up and walked slowly home.

Overcome by their own helplessness, the missionaries wept and prayed long into the night. Had they taught, warned, and pleaded in vain? Would they ever be able to regain footing with so much resentment piled against them? Nonetheless, they had to admit that, from another viewpoint, the opposition might be understandable. Maybe their firm stand against witchcraft did contribute to this lean time—the hunting god holding them responsible.

After that commotion died down, the missionaries met another kind of challenge. Two young Russians fled the Siberian coast one night to escape arrest—whether with good or bad conscience remained uncertain. They set out over the pack ice on foot through fog and rough weather, pushing their way toward freedom. Ten days later they reached the larger island where the natives took them in.

Several days later Little Diomeders heard about the fugitives half-dead from cold, fatigue, and snow blindness. They also knew that their neighbors on the other island had little more than seal meat to eat that time of year. One day the teacher suggested that the Nyseters join them in extending a helping hand toward these refugees who couldn't last long on the limited food supply of Big Diomede.

Gustav quickly agreed. "If you assume responsibility for bringing these foreigners over on American soil, we will take one, and you can take the other."

No law said they couldn't be kind in an emergency such as this. Thus the two famished fellows became their wards, but the following ten weeks became stressful for everyone involved. As soon as the ice opened, Siberian natives came asking about the fleeing Russians. With the Soviets offering generous rewards for their capture, several expeditions followed in hopes of winning the prize. Shaking inwardly as he assumed a position he wasn't sure he had, Gustav put on a brave front. "This is American ground, so don't try to cause trouble here."

It worked. But what if Little Diomeders decided to help the headhunters? That posed another problem. When they could no longer be assured of safety, the two escapees hid among the rocks on the other side of the island. Gustav could only assure the frightened fugitives that, though they were being hunted like animals, none of the locals really dared shoot them.

A passing Coast Guard patrol solved the dilemma by taking the two men to Nome for temporary shelter until proper authorities decided what to do. In the meantime both found work in a gold mine, keeping busy and out of trouble throughout the summer. One of them opened up, admitting he had a godly mother in central Russia who prayed daily for her wayward son.

Suddenly a higher rung on the official ladder ordered the two Russians aboard a government ship for immediate deportation. They looked at each other in disbelief—just when they thought things were going their way! Though unable to help them, a couple of acquaintances promised to stand behind them in prayer. True to their commitment, they spent two solid hours in intercession that a sovereign God would show those young men mercy.

The prisoners boarded the *Northland* as instructed. As it neared the Asiatic coast, the telegrapher sent a wireless ahead, "Can we set two Russians on land here?"

"Do they have passports?"

"No."

"No one comes to land here without a passport."

End of discussion.

The captain approached the fugitives about being put ashore on a desolate spot far removed from Soviet surveillance. How about outfitting them with suitable clothing and as much provision as they wanted?

"It makes no difference," they responded with shrugs. "Sooner or later we'll be found and tortured to death."

A short wave sent from the masthead reached American headquarters. What the young Russians didn't know at the time was that while they waited, their two friends in a small house in Nome again spent the night in prayer.

Finally the ship's radio crackled a message: "Bring the men back to American soil and let them go."

Hallelujah!

Victory on one hand. But at the same time in one of the island huts, Kitikarik lay dying. Often when Gustav brought the elderly widower something to eat he took opportunity to talk about his soul. Kitikarik listened to what the missionary had to say, but chose to hang on to what he considered part of his heritage. Besides, tuberculosis was hastening the end, so what did he have to look forward to?

One day the old man spoke directly of the matter. "Look, I can't go on living like this. My bed is rotting out from under me, and no one can do anything more about it. My brother's child who crawls around in this little room is sure to get my sickness. You must let me kill myself."

"I can't do that," Gustav replied. "You know Laura and I care about you, and we have an extra room now. Wouldn't you like to come to our house, where we could look after you?"

"Yes," he nodded, "that would be good."

"All right. I'll talk to my wife. You know her—happiest when taking care of someone."

Gustav hurried home to talk to Laura, although he already knew what she would say. But when he got back, Kitikarik had changed his mind. Reason? Too weak to brave the bitter cold. Suffice that Gustav carry his heartfelt thanks to Laura for all she had done for him.

When Gustav relayed his message, she cried out in alarm, "Don't you know what that means? You must bring him here."

"No, it would never do to take a dying man out in the cold against his will. Besides, though he seems to have dropped the subject of killing himself, I cautioned the family to watch him carefully."

When Gustav went back the next morning to check on the man, he wasn't there. "He died nine-thirty last night," a family member explained hurriedly.

"How did he happen to die?" he asked a teenager living there.

"He hanged himself."

When Gustav cautiously pried for further information, the girl apparently realized she had blundered. Case closed.

Never had the Nyseters felt demon power so strong as in the spring of 1929. Later they might see themselves as having faced a prelude to the Great Depression, the "crash" that would bring on suicides of desperation on Wall Street. Man, in spite of all his self-preservation instincts, turns on himself as if to rob God of the right to number his days. Worse yet, he steals from the Almighty the joy of calling one of His precious children home. Jesus rose triumphant over the grave so the person who knowingly takes his own life, whether by act or neglect, denies that victory. And the Body of Christ can't help but feel the impact.

To compound the pressures, it seemed that even the elements conspired against them. The island took the brunt of another storm as fierce as the one previously described—perhaps even worse. As a result, the village appointed one of their leaders to talk with the Coast Guard captain when summer came: the Nyseters must leave!

Storms come and go. This one too subsided, and by then the angered spirit had presumably been appeased and gone his way. The matter of ousting the missionaries went along with him. Nonetheless, this and other evidences of rejection were hard to swallow.

With a deep sigh, Gustav approached Laura with what had been on his mind for days. "Shouldn't we try to go back to Norway this coming summer? Eight years. We need to go home."

Her straightforward reply closed further discussion: "Even if you leave, I'll stay here, where the Lord has placed me, until He says 'Go.'"

"But what if it means death?"

"That I can't help. I will be here as long as the Master wills."

On the surface it might appear that Laura acted as head of the house. Gustav, however, didn't take her answer in that light. Instead, he gave her credit for feeling a sense of purpose that he in his weariness had lost. Doing most of the visiting in the village and sharing hurts first hand, he had also become the more frequent target for verbal attacks. Billows of doubt and discouragement broke over him until he felt powerless to take another step. He couldn't go on.

Alone, the man voiced his complaints to the Lord until, having nothing left to say, he listened. While careful lest he blame God for thoughts really his own, he knew when he had finally heard from the Lord. His journal entry read, "Then came that voice that so often calmed life's storms, 'Peace; be still.'

"Jesus! With a renewed sense of His nearness, I felt my entire being relax. He has everything under control. A new and glorious victory was won for myself, for the gospel, for souls bound by chains of sin. Heathen power on Little Diomede received its mortal wound."

22

Shipwrecked Sailors

⸺◆⸺

T he following summer Laura again called Gustav's
attention to their inadequate store of supplies. "You
will need to go to Nome before bad weather closes
in." Not a traveler at heart, she quickly protected herself,
"But I can just as well stay home."

Replenish the larder they must, so Gustav kept his eyes
open for possible transportation to the mainland. Waxing a
bit eloquent, he reminisced how that, over the years, they
had met a number of seafarers, both officers and crews,
from the old country. For the most part those men had always been more than willing to extend a helping hand
whenever possible.

"You know, we stand with a debt of gratitude to them.
God bless our Norwegian seamen!"

Laura smiled. No matter one's nationality, he should
show a sense of loyalty to his own people. That her husband did for sure. Neither was she surprised when the last
of June he came dashing in the house almost out of breath.

"Got to get my bags! There's a hunting schooner out there and the captain said he would gladly take me on board. He's Carl Hansen, the one who had been with Roald Amundsen on the *Maud*. Nome, here I come!"

A one-way ticket did it. He could be gone days, weeks, or even months, with no sure means of getting back. In the meantime anything can happen, especially on Diomede.

While Gustav was away, Laura became part of a story that had begun over a year before. A three-masted power schooner, the *Elisif*, left Seattle on a longer voyage than anyone expected when it pulled away from the pier. An American-owned company had bought the Norwegian vessel for trading purposes, retaining the full crew. The journey as mapped out extended far up the Siberian coast to unload their wares.

By the last of July they had safely passed the Bering Strait when pack ice, that deceitful enemy of ocean traffic, surrounded them. Trapped! Totally unprepared for wintering in the Arctic, the men had no choice but to stay with the ship. For eleven miserably long months they had seen only an occasional small aircraft which braved its way from Nome and once in a while Siberian natives with their dogsleds.

At last, an uncertain lead opened to let the ship pursue its course northward. Though not the direction they wanted, any movement was better than none. As they slowly turned port side, meaning to veer west if possible, a dreaded "mine" (ice hidden below the surface) rammed a gaping hole in the *Elisif's* hull. Immediately the skipper grounded the vessel by turning the wheel toward shallow water. His wise move gave the crew a chance to man the lifeboats. After making sure of their own lives, the sailors fought to salvage whatever they could as gray waves bit and tore at the hull, spitting fragments of great timbers in every direction.

Fifteen men began the long tedious journey back toward civilization in two small open motorboats tied together and crammed with provisions and personal effects. In spite of ice floes and deceptive currents, all went well until they had to again cross the Bering Strait. At that point they encountered a strong southwesterly head on. The small motors performed bravely, bringing their passengers almost to the shelter of Big Diomede when one of the towropes broke. Then, while the men frantically tried to repair their connection, a part of the rope wrapped itself around a propeller.

Helplessly drifting is no idle motion. Swept right back into the main current, and with a diminishing supply of gas, they spent a frightful night tossed about by a raging storm. Not only had they used the last of their food and drinking water but also they were absolutely drenched by salt spray. These experienced seamen weren't kidding themselves—only a miracle could save them.

Hold it! Was a miracle indeed happening? By morning the angry wind seemed to have spent most of its energy. With the unexpected lull came a renewal of hope that somehow they might be rescued. Working frantically, the men finally got the motors started up again. After hours of battling waves and riding breakers, they came to land just below Diomede's schoolhouse.

Imagine their surprise when a tall blonde woman came and spoke to them in their own language! Were they so overcome with fatigue that they imagined a mermaid approaching them? But even in the craziest stories a mermaid doesn't have a cozy little home on dry land to which she invites shipwrecked sailors.

While Laura fired up the stove and prepared a meal, the men removed their sopping wet clothing and tried to get into some of Gustav's clothes. In spite of the dangers they had been through, they had to laugh when a hefty machinist with quite a paunch tried to get into clothes meant to fit a near skeleton (Gustav's own description of himself).

"Out of this world!" one of them exclaimed under his breath as they sat down at a real table to eat. Afterwards, tired bodies stretched out on the floor or on a real bed in a real house with solid ground under them. Laura looked on with pleasure. Never had she seen anyone so appreciative.

The officers and machinists remained in the Nyseters' home, while the ten crewmen slept in the schoolhouse. Their stay on the island came to a quick close the next day when they signaled a passing Coast Guard cutter that took them to the mainland. There they waited weeks before being able to secure passage on a ship bound for Norway. Inasmuch as Gustav also marked time for a couple months in Nome, he spent a lot of hours with these men who had been guests in his home.

Upon finally getting back to Diomede, he and Laura eagerly exchanged stories. Just think! The Lord had given them the privilege of returning in a small way the kindness that seamen over the years had shown them.

"You know what, Laura? He knew we needed to say thank you. And we did."

23

The Cross

⟞⟞⟝

Gustav tallied the years: a winter in Ketchikan, a winter in St. Michael, and six winters on Little Diomede. He felt completely wiped out. God to the rescue, or else....

In his own words, "No one knows the struggle going on in my soul before I could finally say yes to the Lord's request for 'one more year.' It's something I can't talk about as it was strictly between my Lord and me."

He quickly changed the subject. "On the brighter side, I was one happy man setting foot on our island after my prolonged buying trip in Nome. I found my wife as well as she has always been, cheerful, and contented. Together we plunged into getting ready for another winter."

On the second of October the first drift ice eased its way past their shores. Four days later pack ice moved in, forcing Diomede to face the prospect of a tough winter. Besides an extremely limited food supply and a near-empty coal bin in the schoolhouse, a fifth of its population stood stranded on the mainland. Within a few days, however, the threatening expanse of ice withdrew temporarily and along in the afternoon came the *Boxer* from the south. Such excitement! It had hardly dropped anchor before several men climbed on board to unload freight as quickly as possible.

Like a deliberately planned trick, the pack ice sneaked in under cover of night, holding the ship fast until the following day. Taking advantage of the delay, the missionaries got a few more letters ready to go. With a touch of pride they asked a boy to carry the mailbag to the ship before it lifted anchor. Shortly thereafter the island's last contact with the outside world for at least eight or nine months disappeared around the point.

Then came the boy with—could it be? In all the commotion the boy forgot to deliver the big bag of letters! Laugh or cry, it didn't matter either way. Within hours pack ice returned, this time sealing them in for the winter.

The villagers' attitude toward the missionaries took a 180-degree turn, for which the new Eskimo teacher, Samuel Anaruk, and his wife, Beatrice, deserve credit. A beautiful Christian family, the Anaruks were dedicated to serving their own people. Under her father's supervision their sixteen-year-old daughter, Sofie, also filled in capably as teacher for the primary group.

Further, some of the younger folk stood taller than ever, holding their heads up and daring to express their own opinions. Though acting unmoved when Gustav cried out to God for them at the whale dance, they had caught a glimpse of both love and soul anguish on his face. Feeling compelled to complete the dance, they did so. Inwardly, however, they vowed never again to get swept away with undue pressure. Decisions involving right and wrong would be strictly their own.

Harry Soxie, wanting desperately to pick up where his old mentor left off, visited the island in the summer with intentions of extending evangelistic effort in Maritime Siberia. For all his good intentions, he soon had to accept that those doors were closed tight. As an alternative he chose to winter on Diomede, where he rented a house so his wife and daughter could be with him. He preached as never before, and the people listened as never before. They had learned a hard lesson.

The general health of the village seemed to improve, even the weather behaving as if inclined to please. Yes, the winter promised to be one of the best.

A few months later Gustav began a letter home. Some of us might have destroyed it in the end, choosing not to reveal ourselves as less than stalwart in the faith. But, making himself vulnerable, he shared with family and friends the secrets of his heart:

"January 3: A long time has gone by since I last wrote. We have gone through things we really don't understand. After drawing close to the Lord and sensing His nearness more than ever before, we entered a time of severe testing.

"My beloved wife became very sick the end of November and since then has hovered between life and death. Several times she faced the dark valley, but God intervened. Apparently her digestive system refuses to function properly. Over a period of five weeks she has taken no more than what I eat in two meals. She often suffers pain and vomits blood, has difficulty breathing, and her heart is weak. Through it all God has surrounded us with His deep peace, teaching us more of what it means to trust Him.

"The native folk have been most kind, entering into our sufferings to such a depth that I almost feel ashamed. I don't want to be rude, but at last I had to deny them the privilege of visiting my wife any more—her nerves simply can't take it. We have tried to have Bible classes in the living room, but sometimes they, too, have to be dismissed even though we keep the bedroom door closed. Nevertheless, the mission work progresses nicely, thanks to Harry.

"February 14: It's been a long time, but I just couldn't write. There has been a big change in our house since I last wrote. We are now five: Harry Soxie, his wife, and their nineteen-year-old daughter, who gave birth to a son in November. I am the fifth. And what about her who should be the sixth and the light of my life? She has moved far away to a better home, far surpassing anything I could build for her. I will try to tell you more about it.

"The first of December I left my wife alone while I went down to the schoolhouse at the Sunday school hour. This, the work she loved so much, she had to give up, but, to our surprise, toward the end of our session, she came in.

"Asking Harry to interpret for her, she gave a gripping testimony of how God had saved her as a sixteen-year-old girl. She pleaded with all, especially the youth, to come to Jesus and accept His salvation. Afterwards Laura told me that an inner voice had compelled her to go to the meeting. The Lord gave strength as she obeyed Him.

"How can I relate this without sounding contradictory? Afterwards my dear wife became so weak that normal physical rest rarely came, and then only briefly. That unexpected Sunday visit was her last public witness. From then on, what her body endured is difficult for me to describe. I saw a day-by-day miracle that life could hold on in a body so weak, for almost no food passed her lips. What little she tried to take only brought on more pain, but she bore it bravely.

"Alone, taking care of my wife both day and night, I began to get dangerously rundown. One night toward the last I fell as if in a faint. That in turn alarmed her and for days she hardly dared sleep. Seeing how nearly spent I was, she refused to call for help unless in extreme need. Her carefulness, though well meant, made it worse on me.

"The last day she wasn't clear in her mind. Her mouth was swollen and sore; I grasped only fragments of what she said. Along toward evening she regained complete consciousness in spite of a burning fever. Shortly after ten o'clock the next morning, February ninth, she tried to say some words which gradually became clear enough for me to understand—words that did my soul good.

"Hallelujah, Jesus; Hallelujah, Jesus," she repeated over and over again until it flowed in rhythm that I believe was a song. Her breath grew weaker; her voice faded and then was no more.

"The sun sent its first rays through the window at eleven o'clock when her soul took flight to its eternal abiding place. A heavenly peace flooded my own soul and filled the room. It seemed almost a natural gesture to close her eyes and wipe the parched lips—as if she had fallen into blessed sleep. When she wakened we would somehow be together in good health, our futures still before us.

"Harry was having a meeting in the schoolhouse. I walked over to tell the congregation of Laura's departure. Some fought back tears while others followed me home to comfort me. Bernice Anaruk and Harry's wife helped me dress my loved one for the last time. Several who came offered to spend the night, but I thought it best to just be alone with Jesus.

"The next day friends made a coffin. Tuesday we had the funeral, then up that painful, stumbling route I knew all too well to set my dearest down by our Ruth who left us over three years ago. There the two I loved the most will rest until Jesus wakens them, fulfilling the Word of the Lord, "...bring my sons from far, and my daughters from the ends of the earth' (Isa. 43:6).

"As for myself, I stand amazed at the deep settled peace that enveloped my being. Undoubtedly many were praying for me, and certainly my own merciful High Priest by the throne of God intercedes for me. The one who went home asked at the onset of her sickness that, in event of her death, I would carry her last heartfelt greetings to family and friends. The subject of parting we never again mentioned, holding on in hope that God would raise her up. Yet I was aware she prayed for healing only because she knew how difficult it would be for me to be left alone in a distant land. She herself longed to leave this world, to be 'absent from the body, present with the Lord.'

"To think I can thank God for that! How completely selfish if I wished only for my own sake for it to be otherwise. The Lord will give me grace for each day as it comes, whether a short or long time, until I follow her.

"The spiritual aspect here looks brighter than ever. The evening after Laura died, I had a serious talk with shaman Azzekazik, who said he wanted to seek God. The morning before the funeral, nineteen-year-old Olaf came to ask about the way of salvation. We had a precious time together as he gave his young life to Jesus. A day later we had a meeting for inquirers in my home. A number of young people that I have been waiting to see get genuinely converted came—and older folk as well. May God help them make complete commitments to Him. Besides meeting here in the house, we're always available for counseling.

"February 27: The month isn't over. Time drags, partly because I'm sad and this spot seems doubly dreary. I have to remind myself to look upwards when I start getting just plain tired of ice, ice, ice....

"We take advantage of breaks in the weather by going out. I need to stay in shape physically, doing what I can to keep myself in balance. I also realize my sensitive nature could never have made it were it not for the Lord who granted a special portion of His grace and strength.

"Housekeeping isn't the worst. I have enough to eat and enjoy the food others prepare for me. Nevertheless, I question how much longer our present living arrangement can continue as we represent extreme cultural differences. When I asked Harry's family to move in so I wouldn't be overcome with loneliness, I gave them our bedroom. For me a bench in the living room is adequate, only I don't appreciate my makeshift bed being sat on. Sometimes folk come in with soiled parkas.

"Ah, but that's a mighty poor price to pay for bringing souls to Jesus. In return I rejoice seeing first one and then another come over to the Lord's side. We look forward to meetings where we see evidence of the Holy Spirit's working in hearts. What if my own life is broken, if I can but be a sweet fragrance of Christ flowing out to others (2 Cor. 2:15)?

"March 19: How well I remember, exactly five years ago today, crawling through the underground tunnel with our Ruth. As she got older, she'd wave a welcome when she saw me coming. A larger picture of complete family happiness unfolded with the two I loved most waiting for me at home. Home in the fullest sense of the word, even though modest, crowded, and set between boulders on a barren island.

"How little we realized that the tiny being we held so close, like Jonah's gourd, gladdened our hearts only to wither away in two years. We experienced Jonah's hurt, but not his anger. As Laura and I sat alone in our sorrow, we learned anew what it means to draw comfort from God's Word. Many treasured moments were reserved for us two, not least our reading again before the Lord the book of Romans. Was that which we experienced a renewing of our spirits, a recovering from our loss?

"Or was it perhaps a strengthening, a preparation for that which was to come? Sorrow's long night, how God lightened it by His presence! I recall the beautiful, though weak, song that floated now and then from the sick room. Now it belongs to the past, and I stand alone. Only in my sleep is it as if we were still two. 'Home' has become like a foreign word to me. Then I resort to the words of the song, 'This world is not my home.' Praise the Lord, a better place awaits me up there! Walking northward over the ice, I look up to that rocky steep where my two loved ones sleep. With a triumphant smile I burst out, 'Death, where is your sting? Grave, where is your victory?'

"Forgive me that I take so much space just rambling. There's no one here with whom I can share my innermost feelings, and it's too long to wait for some of you to listen. Nevertheless, my young friends here have been a great comfort, perhaps without being aware of it.

"Now, aside from my own sadness, let me tell you about everyday life locally. First about Lila, the headman's nineteen-year-old daughter who five years ago began praying to God with what limited knowledge she had of Him. Later she "married" a boy from the other island. She had never been strong, so everyone feared for her when she waited her first child. It was stillborn. The mother herself passed away between two and three o'clock Sunday morning and by noon the family had already laid her to rest up on the hillside.

"My heart rejoiced upon hearing that Lila firmly refused the shaman's attendance during her illness, for she wanted her soul to be saved. I admit I sob along with the others, but my tears aren't the same as theirs. The pagan family grieves without hope, and for poor William it's all over now. He sits alone, just as I, except for that big difference already mentioned. Bound by superstition, he and his family must spend a month as voluntary prisoners in a gloomy hut. They dare not go hunting, fishing, or take part in other healthy activities after someone in the house has died.

"I confess I'm also troubled for our new converts when I see our youth undependable. I have to correct myself, for we must not expect too much of lives so recently rescued from heathen cellars. Neither is it my right to put old heads on young shoulders. I must be more positive and look at what brings joy.

"Olaf, the first to come as a direct fruit of my wife's admonition when she was sick, is making steady strides forward. So is Sofie, our beginner teacher. Arthur and Fred are likewise gaining ground, but Martha and Helen turned out to be such boy-crazy teenagers. There I go again! Who am I to criticize? I will believe the best for all of them.

"This evening I wanted to serve refreshments for my young friends as this is my wife's birthday. Since we have lots of sea gull eggs, I baked a cake for this special occasion. These faithful believers deserve something extra. Naturally I had to keep this a secret until after the meeting if the treat was to be just for them. Otherwise, I'd have everyone.

"In the house we're getting along fine since we began preparing separate meals. Their customs might be just as good as mine, but we like what we're used to. For example, they sit on the floor while they eat, but that isn't for me every meal. I'll admit they have one advantage—no danger of their toddler pulling off the tablecloth!

"April 1: A biting north wind and bitter cold continue. Not feeling like going out, I occupy myself indoors. There's also prayer and preparation for feeding infants in the faith, a blessed responsibility often blended with tears of love and gratitude.

"How glad I am that Jesus is stronger than Satan! Sunday evening we had a precious prayer meeting in our living room. I almost marvel at these young people. After three gatherings at the schoolhouse earlier in the day, they come here for prayer even though their comrades are organizing a ball game. Monday evening we had a wonderful service with nineteen-year-old Jacob kneeling for prayer—no minor decision with his cousin seated beside him.

"April 14: The weather is so mild that snow melts and drips off the roof, but spring itself is at least a month away. I long for it, yet with a certain dread as I've seen the peculiar effect the changing season has on some of the people. So far though, the good has grown beyond my highest expectation, but I must not give in to discouragement if we hit a slump. The fact that seed may fall on rocky ground cannot be altered; there's bound to be rich soil too, soil that produces to the glory of God.

"In a recent house meeting Olaf told how Jesus came into his life. Afterwards one after another gave their witness just as folk would do in any part of the world. Their words brought both tears and smiles—everyone wanted to say or hear more. In their eagerness these believers asked if they might also share at a regular meeting in the schoolhouse. There, too, testimonies rang clear and true.

"As for me personally, life goes on without incident. But even as people on land cannot see the desperate struggle going on in the deep sea, so with our lives. A battle goes on inside. I'm reacting to all that has happened.

"I ought not to say a word about it, but inasmuch as I may have to stay here until I have 'passed the test,' you have a right to know why I might not come home this summer. At this point I haven't received definite direction from my Lord and King, so perhaps He will keep me here until death's release. I'm ashamed to admit that the very thought of staying leaves me deeply troubled.

"Looking forward to going home to Norway, visiting friends and relatives, buoyed me, gave my broken spirit new courage. But when I began to consider it my duty to squelch these desires, my heart sank—the will to live left me. I lost my appetite and couldn't sleep. Often I felt as if I would smother....

"I began to doubt God's promises. Temptation came and whispered to my soul, 'She died anyway, no matter how much I trusted His word.'

"God blessed our meetings and that helped to back me up. But to die alone here—or worse yet, to lose my mind. That I fear the most. No one I can lean on, no one to help me. Yes, one. JESUS. With that consolation the storm quieted again, at least temporarily. I can't see how I could possibly hold out another year with reminders upon reminders no matter which way I turn.

"I must be a very weak person. Others have given up family and homeland, and without knowing the Lord! Please pray for me that I will remain faithful at my post, even though it be until death.

"May 1: These months called spring are nothing more than a tail of polar winter. When it's foggy and gray as it has been for the last while, it's oppressive. I can't keep from mulling over the clammy, whimsical summer months ahead—and more on the long dark, dismal winter that follows. I try to smile it away, but don't always succeed. So excuse me again—maybe I'm beginning to slip.

"In fairness I must change the subject as there's much to encourage us. Our meetings continue to be uplifting, nor is it unusual to hear testimonies from new converts. Olaf is especially open; his fiancée, Margaret, is quick to express her joy in the Lord. Ten-year-old Susie surprises me too with her public witness.

"Last Sunday we honored the most faithful in Sunday school attendance along with dedicating Naaman, Harry's grandson. A touching scene. Equal cause for rejoicing is the gentle way in which the Holy Spirit is being allowed a greater place in Harry's life. I see now that I've been guilty of feeling sorry for myself while it's been anything but easy for him, my co-worker. Surely God's grace is sufficient for each in his own particular need.

"As a practical Christian witness, two of the larger hunting crews didn't build a small bonfire before the bow of their umiaks at the edge of the ice (a carryover of old superstition). As you might have guessed, Harry and Olaf were part of the crews that sailed free of that kind of fear.

"In contrast, a crew comprised of nonbelievers suffered real losses because of mismanagement. Good came of it when one of the men, Dwight, got laid off work for a day and took the time to look me up. His wife, Martha, had prayed much for him, and he wanted to get right with God. What a joy to lead this young man to the Sinners' Friend. One of his problems was a cigarette habit affecting his eyesight, but this positive decision also put an end to the 'smoke offerings.'

"The water is alive with big sea birds returning north, flocks of them headed on to Siberia. One gray day I sauntered over to South Gate, leisurely watching them. A thick fog bank lay over the top of Big Diomede, not unlike the heavy cloud enveloping my downcast spirit. When the birds came to the cloudbank, they hesitated, flying forth and back, steadily calling to one another. To me their cry sounded like "Tro...tro" [Believe...believe].

"I stood for a long time watching until they finally "believed" their way through the fog. Long after they were out of sight and hearing range, their call of "Tro...tro" echoed in my soul. Why shouldn't I believe? Why shouldn't I hold on in faith in spite of personal fog banks distorting my perspectives and hindering my view of God's bountiful goodness? I praise the Lord for that word of encouragement coming to me through those cranes.

"Winged creatures and walrus came in their season, both providing fresh meat. Otherwise our village food is almost nonexistent, so it's well the three umiaks we spotted coming from Siberia couldn't make it through the ice. Every year it's the same story. They come because they're hungry. 'Worse than ever,' they whine.

"How can I describe them? Plagued with poverty, overcome with their own misery, wrapped in superstition, and downtrodden by Soviet authority. The saddest part: the majority still grope without honestly reaching for the light.

"How thankful we are to be on this side of the strait, even if springtime offers a combination of both new energy and real drowsiness. Though these new converts are still happy in the Lord, they're often so tired they fall asleep as soon as they sit down. They have reason—out hunting forty-eight to seventy-two hours in a stretch. We're indeed grateful they take advantage of every opportunity to fellowship with other believers.

"I gave my guitar, my trusty friend that followed me through thick and thin for over twenty years, to Dwight who will soon be able to play for the meetings. I'm using my wife's guitar. Both instruments bear plainly the marks of time, just as I do, but they and I can say of many of these scars that they were added to us for Jesus' sake.

"The snow has begun to melt from the stony crag, so some day this week I can set up a cross made of one-inch planks painted white and carved with gilded letters. She whose tired body rests there deserves a better marker, but it's the best I can do with material on hand.

"June 14: Time goes quickly now. If I could only forget my own hurt it would be great. Living with a family, household activities going on around me, has been good. Harry's little grandson and I are the best of friends.

"It appears that this winter determined to set a record for longevity. Old pack ice holding its own hinders our contact with the outside. New snow rests on the high point of our island while new ice forms around us every night. It wouldn't matter if it weren't for our hungry neighbors constantly begging for bread or flour. Unfortunately, we haven't much left. Between visits I shed tears for them, realizing that matters might not improve right away. The people aren't starving, but it's hard after they have become accustomed to better fare. Children can't understand the meaning of doing without, so for them this shortage is tough.

"I've tried to fix up around the graves of my two loved ones. When I found a spot among the stones by the larger grave, I prepared the ground for another coffin somewhat longer.... But the place remains empty as long as this hand can write. I might add that I'm well as I've ever been physically, but my desire to live is gone.

"Counting on sending mail before long, I'll close this long portrayal of winter. I know it's not well written and too much space is taken up with my own feelings. Let's be honest—the lines may be bad, but if you could read between the lines, it's even worse. I wrote as I went along; it would have been different had I written all at once.

"I won't make excuses. I only plead that you not criticize me too severely. Please remember that a broken heart and shattered hopes dictated much of this letter. Even John the Baptist, greatest born of woman, had to go through his battle behind prison walls. I trust that, like him, I have faithful friends who will talk to Jesus for me. They will hold up the hands that only want to hang down.

"June 23: At last, a ship in sight. The Coast Guard boat, *Northland*, steers toward our island. It is well that I didn't send this letter earlier, for now I can close with a lighter note.

"The battle has been tough, but a will to live surfaced in spite of my being so blue that I considered my own burial up among the boulders. Besides, something within me always protested against dying on Diomede, even though I got ready just in case. For two and a half months this up-and-down battle raged, absolutely wearing me down. I was so shaken up and nervous that I decided to hide myself up in the cliffs as soon as I saw a ship. I couldn't face anyone from the outside world.

"But the change has come. Several hours each day with my Bible and with my Jesus has restored my faith in the good old promises. The Lord's words were sweet to my soul. I drank of living water and my spirit was restored. Oh, what relief to lay my struggles down and simply rest in Him! I experienced the truth of Psalm 30:11, 'Thou hast turned for me my mourning into dancing: thou hast put off my sackcloth, and girded me with gladness.' Praise the Lord! Dead or alive, Diomede or Norway—choices that are no longer important. I have Jesus!

"Also, outwardly we see a change. The ice has gone, and we have nice summer weather. On June 19 a skin boat came back from Prince of Wales with lots a mail—a real encouragement to me. Four Siberian umiaks have come too. It's as if they come from another world. Poor people, so unhappy. 'Worse then ever' their continued story.

"I have just been on board the Coast Guard cutter. No problem to meet outsiders now—I could shake hands with President Hoover without it phasing me. The captain expressed his deepest sympathy over my loss and will come again to take me to Nome if that be my wish. As the Lord wills.

"Over the ship's telegraph we hear that a number of vessels are heading toward the Bering Strait. It will be lively around here.

"With that I close this long journal.

"Yours kept by the grace of Jesus, Gustav."

"July 1: The past two weeks have been restful—my own personal storm is over. With the calm came that sense of divine guidance I had been waiting for—to go home to Norway. One of the Scriptures the Holy Spirit made especially clear for me the last of June was, 'Return unto the land of thy fathers, and to thy kindred; and I will be with thee' (Gen. 31:3). Interestingly, my heart remained quiet even with such a glad word. Whatever He might have said would be all right. Content with Jesus alone.

"Again I must get ready for a long journey. Easily done as there's not much I want to take home with me. Harry will be responsible for the house as well as for the work until other missionaries come to take over. I appreciate his dependability.

"A number of errands here and there, then everything is in order for departure. When Captain Pedersen came with his trading vessel on July first, he expressed sincere sympathy—real compassion for me in my loss. As soon as he could find opportunity for us to talk in confidence, he said he would be glad to take me to Nome. It wouldn't cost me a cent. With heartfelt thanks I accepted his offer.

"At 2:00 A.M. the second of July, trading with the villagers was done. Time for the ship to weigh anchor. I said farewell to my dear people—and up at the special place among the boulders. Then the last handshakes with those who shove off in their skin boats. I climbed to the top deck for one last look over the scene that had become so much a part of me. Against the clear morning light the cross stands out on a high point.

"Listen. Is that her voice? 'You get to go home, while I remain on this lonely isle.'

"No, she isn't there—just her house of dust. That moment, however, I'll never forget....

"The propeller begins to turn as the ship moves slowly toward the south end of the island.

"Farewell, Diomede. Farewell, earth's end."

Cross on Laura Nyseter's grave; Big Diomede in background.

Til mine om henne som trofast stod på
sin post ved jordens ender til døden avløste—
Laura Nyseter
(fodt Volden)
er denne bok skrevet.

Translated from Gustav Nyseter's original work:

This book is dedicated to the memory of
Laura Volden Nyseter,
who stood steadfast in her call to the earth's farthest ends
until death released her.

Epilogue

Half a century after Gustav Nyseter returned to his native country, I had the privilege of reading and translating his book, *Earth's Farthest Ends*. Then, needing to get the feel of the island that meant so much to him, I became one of three passengers in a small ski plane landing on the Bering Strait ice. To the west lay Big Diomede, to the east Little Diomede.

Small frame houses looked at first glance like boxes stacked in mild disarray against a steep ragged hillside. A modern school-gymnasium complex caught our attention, but only momentarily. Farther up the hill stood a white cross, the focal point of our visit.

The next day we climbed the rugged steep, careful lest our feet slip off the rocks and get wedged in deep crevices cutting into the core of the mountain. Nearby weathered grave markers leaned awkwardly, were broken, or had toppled over. This one cross, however, defied every storm that beat against it.

"Gales up to a hundred miles an hour can make the strongest building tremble. Then why has this cross stood so long?" I asked.

"Because," an old-timer explained, "Mr. Nyseter preserved the wood by first saturating it with oil. We may touch up the paint occasionally, but the oil went to the heart, penetrating every fiber."

Obviously, the marker could not be secured in the meager surface layer of soil on the mountainside, but again love found a way. Gustav nailed the upright beam to the headboard of the pine box, later placing huge stones against it for added support.

"When we want to line up something in the village," the local resident added, "we can line it up with the cross because it stands absolutely true."

In winter, its white stands out against nature's white; in summer, against her greens; in spring and fall, against her brown and gray. Clearly visible to lonely outposts on Big Diomede, it has stood through years of Soviet domination as a silent witness to the faith of those who loved not their lives unto death.

Now, over sixty years later, the dream of the Nyseters and their contemporaries bid fair to come true. Hearing the glad tidings in Heaven, they rejoice that the Good News is once again being heard in the Russian Far East. Some of the bearers of that news are the spiritual children and grandchildren of earlier heroes of the faith. The people they loved so dearly, and for whom they gave so much, carry the work forward that others might avoid the broad path leading to destruction. Buoyed by the prayers of those who have a burden for the north, they make their way over Bering barriers.

On the opposite shore they were welcomed by mainlanders who had recalled early visitors like Nyseter, Høijer, and Soxie. If too young themselves to have remembered, they know them from storytellers who in fond memory preserved the names of those who had proven that the gospel message is one to be believed and received.

The message is simple. There stands yet another cross of far greater significance than the one on Diomede, for time can never alter it. Anointed with the oil of the Holy Spirit, anchored in the supreme sacrifice paid at Calvary, that cross holds absolutely true.

It stands at the entrance of the strait gate, the gate that leads to salvation and life eternal.

Bibliography

Amundsen, Roald. *My Life as an Explorer*. Doubleday, 1928, New York, NY.

Bills, Paul. *Alaska*. Gospel Publishing House, 1980, Spring field, MO.

Hauge, Halvdan. *Oscar Brown*. Norway: Luther Forlag, 1979, Oslo, Norway.

Hulley, Clarence C. *Alaska 1741–1953*. Binsford & Mort, 1953, Portland, OR.

Maakestad, J. L. *The Lutheran Church in Alaska*. Ken Wray's Print Shop, Inc., 1978, Anchorage, AK

Martinson, Ingeman. *Maste Man Lyde Gud*. Sweden: Slaviska Missionens Forlag, 1973, Bromma, Sweden.

McCracken, Harold. *God's Frozen Children*. Doubleday, 1930.

Nyseter, Gustav. *Jordens Ytterste Ender*. Kvina Trikk (reprint), 1976, Kvinesdal, Norway.

Rasmussen, Knud. *Across Arctic America*. G. P. Putnam's Sons, 1927; Greenwood Press, 1969, New York, NY.

Thomas, Tay. *Cry in the Wilderness*. Mrs. Lowell Thomas, Jr., 1967, Anchorage, AK.

If not available through your local bookstore you may
order additional copies of

STRAIT GATE

by sending $10.99 plus shipping and handling to

Books, Etc.
PO Box 4888
Seattle, WA 98104

or have your credit card ready and call

(800)917-BOOK